Praise for Lessons from Abdul

"With *Lessons from Abdul,* leaders learn to approach every encounter with a mindset of learning and openness." —**Cy Wakeman,** *New York Times* **best-selling author and global thought leader**

"Robb Holman's insights lead readers to find wisdom in unexpected places and diverse encounters." —**Ellen Rogin,** *New York Times* **best-selling author**

"*Lessons from Abdul* delivers transformative principles to awaken your higher purpose and selflessly serve others." —**Marcel Schwantes, international speaker, author, and global employee engagement influencer**

"Embark on a profound transformation! Robb Holman's latest book ignites curiosity and fosters self-discovery through genuine and selfless receiving." —**Dr. Marshall Goldsmith, Thinkers50 #1 executive coach and** *New York Times* **best-selling author of** *The Earned Life, Triggers,* **and** *What Got You Here Won't Get You There*

"Inside our hearts, we hold the power to learn from others, which is one of life's greatest gifts. When we embrace this gift, it can lead us to places we never thought were possible." —**Chris Singleton, inspirational speaker, award-winning author**

"Life and basketball share a profound similarity—both are exceptional teachers. Yet it's mentors like Abdul who hold the power to offer transformative wisdom to those open to receiving it." —**David Kiley, United States Olympic and Paralympic Hall of Famer, Class of 2022, and nine-time Paralympic Gold Medalist**

"Leaders must be learners. In this book, Robb shares his own captivating odyssey of personal growth as he acquires wisdom from an unconventional mentor." —**Cheryl Bachelder, former CEO of Popeyes Louisiana Kitchen, Inc., author of *Dare to Serve***

"For a leader to understand and embrace the values of their organization, they need to first know their own values. This book will inspire and teach you how to live and lead with a strong sense of purpose and a focus on serving others." —**Howard Behar, President of Starbucks, retired**

"Robb Holman's latest book, *Lessons from Abdul*, is essential reading for leaders who want to grow their influence and show up every day for their teams. Robb's vivid storytelling, coupled with his encouraging words, show the power of what it looks and feels like to lead and how empowerment and learning look in real time—as well as what it means to receive others authentically. This is next-level leadership from one of the great experts of our time. Absolutely transformational." —**Dr. Brad Shuck, Professor of Leadership, University of Louisville**

"A profound and pure space is touched within our hearts as we embrace the wisdom offered in this book." —**Aref Dostyar, Senior Advisor on Afghanistan at the Kroc Institute for International Peace Studies, University of Notre Dame, and Former Consul General of Afghanistan in Los Angeles**

"The book's selfless posture teaches the true essence of receiving and its impact on personal and leadership development."—

Monte Williams, Executive Coach & Leadership Expert

"Robb empowers readers on how to develop their leadership that transcends from just working, but in serving others through the lessons learned from leaders in life!" —**Jasmine Romaine, International Keynote Speaker, Global Woman Award Honoree and Best Selling Author of** *Speak to Profit: Speak with Confidence and Jazz Up Your Sales*

"I have always heard it is better to give than to receive, and *Lessons from Abdul: The Hidden Power of Receiving from Anyone, Anytime* has given me a completely new perspective on that concept and an aspect of leadership I never really considered. Robb masterfully delves into the often-overlooked importance of "receiving" in leadership, challenging conventional wisdom with compelling anecdotes and well-reasoned arguments. The balance between giving and receiving is presented as a critical element for authentic human connections and effective leadership. The book is a must-read for anyone looking to deepen their understanding of leadership dynamics and personal growth. It's a transformative read that will change how you approach relationships, both professionally and personally." — **Steven Robertson, keynote speaker and author of Aliens Among Us: 10 Surprising Truths about Gen Z**

"When leaders are ingrained to give and teach, are they primed for receiving?" Robb Holman brings a captivating and fresh perspective on the benefits for leaders to be open, aware and willing to receive from others. Insightful, original and timely. — **Kathi Balasek, Founder & CEO Grief Smart Professional**

"Robb Holman's thought-provoking book is the guide we all desperately need to fully embrace our unique identity. This is an inspirational self-discovery journey with a fresh perspective on elevated ways to lead and live." — **Stephen VanValin, Author**

III

of The Search for Meaning at Work

"Finding a mentor on the fringe is one key discipline leaders can practice to help broaden their horizons and deepen their character. Robb's latest book will help you learn things no one else is teaching because you'll learn to curiously go for development to places where no one else is going."— **David Achata, Author, Executive Coach, Cultivating Clarity for Leaders and Organizations**

"Holman does it again! He provided another book that challenges you to think differently about who you are and how you show up both at work and home. He proves that great leaders can receive from anyone, anytime. It's how they build trust, embrace diversity, and unlock growth." — **Justin Patton,** *Founder of The Trust Architect Group*

"What a powerful book and a beautiful testament to Abdul Ford-Bey's amazing mentorship and impact. Read Lessons From Abdul if you want to learn how to receive more deeply so you can give more expansively. Here, Robb draws on his unique background to help us boost our capacity to give (and love) while fostering a new cycle of generosity that propels your leadership and impact to the highest heights." — **Kathy Caprino, global career and leadership coach, speaker/trainer, Finding Brave host, and author of Breakdown, Breakthrough and The Most Powerful You.**

"What a refreshing look at servant leadership in *Lessons from Abdul*! The concept of 'receiving deeply in order to give greatly' will resonate with modern leaders who recognize that they must first improve themselves before being able to take their organization to the next level. Add this book to your leadership library." — **Bernard K. Nunies, Chief Human Resources Officer, Tradewind Group**

"Lessons from Abdul is a brilliantly insightful lesson and reminder for any leader, helper, caregiver, or individual. Robb Holman reminds us that many leaders struggle with receiving, but if you only give, and no one receives, it doesn't work! Robb draws the often missed connection that a lack of receiving can shift power dynamics, that can lead to organization cultures where we just don't feel we belong. 'Lessons from Abdul' invites the reader to discover their true authentic self, so that they can become the best contributor, the best family member, the best teammate, and the best version of themselves. Holman shares a ton of practical wisdom, and easy to apply tools to help anyone show up as the best version of themselves. Regardless of where you are on your growth journey, *Lessons from Abdul* can help you reach another level in your life." — **Stan Peake, bestselling author, TEDx speaker, and executive coach**

LESSONS *from* ABDUL

The Hidden Power of Receiving from
Anyone, Anytime

ROBB HOLMAN

ISBN 979-8-9897461-1-8 Paperback

ISBN 979-8-9897461-2-5 Hardback

Holman International Press

I dedicate this book to Abdul Ford-Bey—my coach, my mentor, and my friend. You are the man who made my childhood dream of playing professional basketball come true, but more importantly, you are the person who showed me qualities within myself that I couldn't see on my own. Thank you for modeling the power of selfless service. You're all heart, Ab!

Contents

Introduction

During a flood, a man prayed to God for help. When a neighbor in a canoe, a rescue team in a boat, and a helicopter arrived to save him, he refused, expecting God to intervene directly. Tragically, he drowned. In heaven, he asked God why he wasn't saved. God replied, "I sent you help through your neighbor, the rescue team, and the helicopter. What more did you expect?"

Whether you are a person of faith or not, this familiar story encompasses various lessons. But one of its key messages revolves around the importance of being receptive to receiving from anyone at any time. By embracing a posture of openness and a willingness to learn rather than focusing solely on what we can give, we create opportunities for greater success for ourselves and others.

Think about it this way. If everyone only gave and no one received, how would that work?

Leaders and others often find it hard to accept help, compliments, and different viewpoints. In *Lessons from Abdul*, I talk about seven main reasons leaders struggle with receiving and share ten important lessons I learned from my unlikely mentor. These can help you overcome your challenges.

When you learn to receive well, you become a better giver, too, making a positive impact on others.

My personal journey of learning from this unconventional mentor not only highlights the potential of gaining wisdom from anyone but also demonstrates that by embracing new perspectives, you can unlock profound personal growth!

Unlike the man who cried out to God and seemingly received no help, I was fortunate to uncover a profound inner willingness to learn from someone who was very different from me.

By exploring this shared experience, I want to show how important it is to have an open mindset and a tender heart. That will help us discover more about ourselves, find our purpose, and truly inspire others.

Robb Holman

Holman International

Founder and Chief Inspiration Officer

www.robbholman.com

Part I

Purpose Empowers Greatness

CHAPTER 1

Discover the Power Within for Lasting Success

When I learn to respect myself, then I can learn to respect everyone else.

—Abdul

As I walked into the gym before my local youth basketball game started, I heard the strong voice of one of the coaches. It instantly grabbed my attention. The tone of his voice was powerful and passionate as he shouted at the players and gave even louder instructions.

As a 10-year-old, I found myself both captivated and intimidated.

I soon discovered that the source of this commanding voice was a middle-aged African American man with a scraggly beard and loose, curly hair. He had a compelling presence and was wearing a faded tee, dark-rimmed glasses, rolled-up jeans, and a pair of Chuck Taylors.

I was a pretty good player in that local YMCA basketball league and often found my name mentioned in the newspaper. But to my shock, the writer consistently spelled my name wrong. That always bothered me. Imagine being repeatedly called Rod instead of Robb. That's not good for a young ego! To my surprise, the man who wrote those newspaper articles was the very same man who consistently shouted from the sidelines. His weekly column recapped the weekend's games.

Holman powers Biddy JV Rockets

Rob Holman tossed in 15 points to lead the Rockets over the Bucks, 21-8, in Phoenixville Area YMCA Biddy Basketball junior varsity action last Saturday at the Family Center gym.

lead in the final session themselves with turno\ Kings got a couple of key the end to pull away.

Chuck Romig bolstered

His name was Abdul.

Fascinated by Abdul's interesting personality, I started asking my teammates about this man and his story. Many of them mentioned his unusual coaching philosophy and background—loud voice, working multiple sports-related jobs. Eventually, he approached me and my older brother, extending us an invitation to join his team. Although hesitant, I mustered the courage to accept. Little did I know that this decision would mark an extraordinary journey—a journey that would profoundly impact my inner being.

But it wasn't easy.

I was nervous.

I was apprehensive.

I was afraid.

My fear was because that person on the sidelines was outside my comfort zone, and we seemed to have little in common. I was 10; he was 40. I was an upper-middle-class white kid; he was a lower income African American man. I was Christian; he was Muslim. I wore trendy clothes; he wore older clothes. That created a sense of vulnerability in my willingness to receive from him.

Would I be able to open myself up enough to receive from this man who was so different from me? Would I be able to connect with him? Learn from him? Improve under his leadership?

I know I'm not alone in this. I think most people find it challenging to receive from individuals who are different from them, especially when those people are vastly different. Leaders—especially in business for the purposes of this book—face this scenario every day. Although their natural tendencies and training have reaped some wonderful rewards, they often stop short of the true exchange necessary for a genuine connection in human-to-human relationships.

Leaders interact with all kinds of people every day. Typically, they are on the giving end, sharing their time, resources, and energy within their sphere of influence in order to build and sustain people and their work. Many leaders have a natural inclination to give. In the article "How Our Brains Make Us Generous," Summer Allen and Jill Suttie present groundbreaking neuroscience studies that build on prior discoveries, indicating that humans possess an inherent, almost instinctive, inclination to assist others.

But what about receiving? Are we willing to receive from those who are vastly different than us—people with a different culture, a different religion, a different social status? We find it easy to give to all people, but are we open to receiving what those same people have to offer? Think of it this way. If everyone is busy giving, who's available to receive the blessings that others provide?

In the workplace, there is a significant emphasis on giving. But I am committed to bringing a much-needed balance to the workplace—a balance of giving and receiving. This is where my journey with Abdul comes in. Abdul had much to give, and I had to be willing to receive it—no matter our differences.

It's important to clarify that when I say "receiving," I am not referring to "taking" or attempting to manipulate people, circumstances, or situations for personal gain. Receiving is distinct from those things; it involves experiencing genuinely and deeply what another person freely gives. The balance between giving and receiving is a beautiful thing. And more than a balance, it's a fusion of the two.

I like how John Amodeo, author of *Dancing with Fire: A Mindful Way to Loving Relationships*, describes it:

> *The parched earth can't let in a life-giving rain if it is covered by plastic tarp... Without the capacity to be touched by caring and appreciation, we render these gifts less meaningful. Sacred receiving, letting things in with heartfelt gratitude, is a gift to the giver! When we are visibly moved, it conveys that they've made a difference in our lives. We may then bask together in a non-dual moment in which there is no distinction between the giver and the receiver. Both people are giving and receiving in their own unique ways. This shared experience can be profoundly sacred and intimate—a moment of delectable grace.*

Breaking Barriers: The Hidden Power of Receiving

You can only give what you have received.

The premise underlying my first three books—the *Inside Out Leadership* trilogy that includes *Lead the Way*,

All In, and *Move the Needle*—centers on the notion that you can only give what you have received. Devoting my life's work to assisting others, I aim to empower leaders to embrace their authentic identity and purpose, enabling them to generously share their gifts with others.

I have encountered many leaders who are known for their generosity and ability to give. However, I've also experienced others who give with a selfish motive, expecting something in return. Regardless, both types of leaders tend to avoid being in the "receiving spotlight," fearing that it might be perceived as a sign of weakness. Being open to receiving can be seen as an act of vulnerability, which is something leaders often try to avoid. While receiving can empower the giver, it is generally not something leaders prefer from their perspective. Because of this weakness, they find it difficult to consider different viewpoints or incorporate them into company culture.

Looking back at the beginning of my journey with Abdul, I realize now that it was a blessing that I hadn't progressed too far before his involvement. I hadn't relied too heavily on my default mechanism of giving or ignored the benefit of receiving. If I had, that could have hindered my ability to fully embrace and continue on this explorative journey with Abdul.

It's worth mentioning that receiving generally fits into these three categories: (1) receiving praise or compliments, (2) dealing with different viewpoints or opinions, and (3) accepting help and support (I'll explain this in greater detail in Chapter 7, "Silent Strength Radiates"). And in order to truly receive, we must overcome our natural inclination to give. Before we delve into this further, it's essential to explore seven primary reasons why receiving from those very different from us is often challenging.

#1 Hurt Can Hold Us Back

In her insightful article in *Psychology Today*, Kimberly Key sheds light on the matter:

> *When our hearts have been wounded, we may instinctively shield ourselves by developing a hardened exterior. This self-protective mechanism can make genuine intimacy seem risky. By only focusing on giving and not allowing ourselves to receive, we create an obstacle that impedes the free flow of love. Any obstruction in this flow prevents us from fully experiencing the beauty of love.*

#2: The Path of Least Resistance

If we're not careful, we can find ourselves surrounded by what I call mini-me's—individuals and groups who share similar interests, passions, educational backgrounds, life experiences, and values. Such people justify and echo our opinions and thought processes. It is natural for us to subconsciously gravitate toward those who are similar to us, and we find it challenging to receive from individuals who are different.

#3 Letting Go of Control

When we give, we are in a position of control. We have the power to decide how much we give, how we give, and to whom we give. We are in total control of the act of giving. But when we receive something, it puts us in a vulnerable position, and the only thing we control is the ability to refuse the offer. It's like getting a gift we didn't expect. In accepting the gift, we know we didn't do anything to earn it.

#4 Fear of Conditions Placed on Giving

People often instinctively believe there must be a hidden motive behind a giver's actions. We are so accustomed to the notion of "I'll scratch your back if you scratch mine" or "now you owe me" that we erect barriers when it comes to receiving. We yearn for unconditional generosity but hesitate to believe that something so good can be true. If we do receive, we often feel compelled to reciprocate, perpetuating an unhealthy cycle.

#5 Moral Guidelines, Faith-Based Principles

Many of us have been raised with the belief that giving is more important and meaningful than receiving. However, such teaching is only part of the story. The other often neglected part of the story is that what we have to give is almost always an accumulation of the many contributions and gifts that others have given us. We have placed an excessive emphasis on giving and thus overlooked the importance and necessity of receiving. This mindset has frequently left us burdened with guilt when faced with the opportunity to receive. In some cases, we may even deny ourselves the possibility of embracing the act of receiving.

#6: Unveiling the Noble Mask

Some people may struggle with accepting positive feedback due to a fear that it might inflate their ego (if coming from a superior) or make them appear weak or vulnerable (if coming from a subordinate). As a result, they deflect praise from others. While this behavior may appear noble on the surface, it can mask deeper issues related to a lack of self-understanding and purpose. It suggests that those individuals may have allowed external influences to shape their identity and define their perception of success.

#7: The Paradox of Closeness

When you become overly familiar with the idiosyncrasies, imperfections, and temperament of your inner circle, it can pose challenges to receiving from them. I'm reminded of the old adage, "Familiarity breeds contempt."

Take a moment to reflect on the barriers that have historically hindered you from fully receiving from others, particularly those who are different from you. If you're still reading this, it suggests that you are, at the very least, curious and perhaps even ready to embark on the most transformative *Inside Out Leadership* journey of your life. This journey requires tapping into the depths of your authentic self while embracing your experiences and where you've been. It echoes your creative curiosity, much like my own initial journey with Abdul. Remember, it's never too late to reconnect with the childlike wonder within you!

As you embark on this exploration, remember that you hold the keys to **your own heart** as a gatekeeper. It's not about receiving *everything all the time* but rather learning how to open **yourself** up to receiving from *anyone anywhere*. Overcoming big barriers and receiving and embracing genuine humility in the process requires acknowledging a universal truth that when we approach receiving with childlike openness, there is a purity and authenticity that goes beyond any sense of deserving. The most precious and fulfilling aspects of life are free—free from conditions, accusations, manipulation, and judgment. Imagine the impact we could make if we tapped into the innocence and power of receiving from anyone anytime, and in our giving, gave from that place of abundance.

The #1 Leadership Thinker
Transformed through Receiving

On my *Inside Out Leadership* podcast, I've had the honor of interviewing some of the world's greatest inside-out leaders. These exceptional individuals hail from various fields such as business, sports, politics, and entertainment. They have consistently demonstrated inspiration, humility, courage, perseverance, and servant leadership. In other words, they are extraordinary givers. Throughout the rest of this book, you will have the opportunity to hear from some of these remarkable leaders.

During these interviews, I have delved into the inner work of each leader and explored how their inner work has contributed to their outer work of influence. One of those interviews was with Marshall Goldsmith, a member of the Thinkers50 Hall of Fame and the number-one leadership thinker in the world. What struck me most about this incredibly giving individual was what he shared about the most impactful time of his life—his experience in Africa in 1985 with the Family Relief Campaign.

During that nine-day trip, Marshall accompanied an NBC film crew to witness the global hunger crisis. He shared that it was a profound and sobering experience to see people starving. A picture from that trip, which he included in his book *Triggers*, captures a line of children and a woman measuring their arms. If their arms were too small, they received no food; they were sent away.

If their arms were too big, they were deemed not hungry enough and also received no food. Only those whose arms were in the middle received nourishment.

Marshall kept that picture as a daily reminder to be grateful for what he had—from what he had received. In his own words, "If someone's going to improve, it's only going to come from one place and one place alone—in their heart." Marshall learned the importance of receiving deeply, and the experience changed him profoundly. It touched him at the core and enabled him to give even more of his heart and success to others. It was a transformation that forever shaped him. It allowed him to understand the profound impact of receiving and how it can fuel our ability to give.

Reflecting on Marshall's experience of receiving, I am grateful for the reminders in my own life that success is an inside job. Much like Marshall, I have kept pictures that serve as powerful reminders of the importance of staying connected to my inner journey as I navigate the ongoing process of receiving and growing.

And yes, you will come across some of those cherished reminders—pictures and stories of Abdul—woven into the pages of this book.

How a Higher Perspective Facilitates Receiving

"Dad, I'm happy for the opportunity to play a grade above my actual grade!" That was my daughter's heartfelt response midway through the traveling basketball season after experiencing a shift from being a starter with significant playing time (playing at grade level) to being on the bench with limited minutes in the game (a grade above).

As a father and former professional basketball player, my heart sank. And after that specific game, it sank even farther. I felt frustration and discouragement, not for myself but for my 11-year-old daughter. As we headed to the car to grab a snack, I shared my heart with her, hoping to understand. I asked her how she felt, and to my surprise, she responded, "I'm a bit frustrated, but I'm really thankful for the chance to play in a higher grade."

It was in that instant that I marveled at my daughter's insight. How could someone so young with limited life experiences respond with such a positive mindset? She had discovered that true success doesn't rely solely on external factors but rather is an inside job. It necessitates an internal perspective that guides our ability to receive.

After that conversation, I witnessed a remarkable transformation in my daughter's approach to the game. Her risk-taking mirrored my own experience of joining Abdul's team. Just as she chose to stay committed and maintain an inner perspective of gratitude, I, too, faced similar challenges when I made the decision to play on Abdul's team despite my initial uncertainties.

We both discovered that true success lies not only in

the external outcomes but also in the unwavering belief in ourselves and perhaps something or someone greater than us. It takes courage to navigate through difficult situations, to stay committed to a path despite setbacks, and to maintain an inner perspective that transcends external circumstances.

As the basketball season progressed, my daughter's renewed mindset and unwavering dedication began to pay off. Her game improved, and her contributions became instrumental in her team's success. And my courage to step onto Abdul's team eventually led to my personal growth and triumph on the court.

In the next chapter, we'll talk about how embracing your inner north star will help you break barriers and set you up to receive success.

Lesson #1

Discover the Power Within through Self-Awareness

To authentically receive from others and position ourselves as genuine receivers, we must acknowledge the innate power within us that paves the way for lasting success. It begins by nurturing our deepest selves through healthy self-awareness, gaining a higher perspective, and cultivating unwavering confidence. I discuss all these topics in this book, and I explored them in greater depth in my first three books—*Lead the Way, All In,* and

Move the Needle. These essential elements enable us to open up and wholeheartedly embrace the transformative potential that comes with receiving.

4 Key Takeaways

1. There is transformative power in embracing vulnerability and opening ourselves up to receiving from individuals outside our comfort zone. When we step outside the familiar and allow ourselves to be vulnerable, we create opportunities for growth and profound transformation.

2. Understanding the reasons behind our resistance to receive is the first required step to break free from limitations, heal past wounds, and cultivate genuine intimacy, ultimately enriching our relationships and experiences.

3. Receiving deeply has a big impact on our ability to give and how we see the world. It can change us in a powerful way and make us more generous toward others.

4. True success extends beyond mere external outcomes and is intricately tied to our inner well-being and belief in ourselves. It may also involve recognizing the presence of something or someone greater than us, whether it is a higher power, a guiding force, or a supportive network of individuals.

Reflection

- On a scale of 1 to 10 (1 is the lowest, 10 is the highest), how effectively are you opening yourself up to receiving from people who are very different from you?

- Think of the most recent time you opened yourself up to someone who was very different from you. How did you feel? How did you manage to establish a connection with them? What were the results?

- Describe what skills you use to spot opportunities in tough situations.

CHAPTER 2

Embrace Your Inner North Star

The courage to be one's own natural self is quite a rare thing.

—*Abdul*

To the best of my recollection, during one of my first practices with Abdul, he shouted so loudly that it startled one of my teammates—and he peed his pants.

As I mentioned in the last chapter, I was intimidated by this coach but felt drawn to him at the same time. How could someone who looked and acted so differently from me share the same level of passion for the game I had dedicated my early life to?

"Hit the floor!" he yelled. "Get the chairs out!" "It's time to play slap-back!" These were just a few of the phrases he frequently used during practice, ones he had probably been using throughout his entire coaching career. But for me, they were completely new.

"Cricket," he called out to one player. "Grasshopper," he said to another. "Gumby," he shouted to a third. These were nicknames he had given the players who had been with him before. But since I didn't have a nickname, I felt like an outsider. However, as you will soon learn, that feeling didn't last long.

With this new, unorthodox coach came a whole new basketball language and culture. I was completely overwhelmed and scared. But I still kept coming back to practice. I was intrigued, open, and eager to learn more.

It felt like I had entered a new world, one that was completely different from anything I had experienced before. And at the center of it was a man who couldn't be any more different than me.

Discovering Your Inner North Star: Unveiling Your Unique Identity and Purpose

My first encounter with Abdul was nerve-wracking, and my hesitancy and apprehension continued as I embarked on this new journey. Despite the barriers holding me back that I shared in Chapter 1, I found the courage to press forward. What gave me that courage? It was the ability to embrace my inner north star.

In simpler terms, it means understanding your unique identity so you can live a purposeful and meaningful life—free to receive from others who are different. This concept is at the core of my first book, *Lead the Way,* where I take leaders on a journey to discover or rediscover their personal purpose. It involves answering important questions about who you are.

The first aspect is knowing the **Who**. To understand why you exist, you must embrace your unique identity. Consider these five questions:

- *What are your core values?* These deep convictions guide your daily decisions.

- *What are your top strengths?* These natural talents hold great potential.

- *What are your greatest passions?* They are the things that excite you and energize you.

- *What are your most impactful life milestones?* These positive or challenging experiences have shaped you.

- *What is your primary gift?* It is the unique legacy you leave behind.

While embracing your inner north star covers various aspects of your identity, I want to focus on your core values since they serve as both an anchor and a source of liberation when it comes to receiving from others.

Once you affirm your unique identity, you can move on to the **What**. This involves finding a problem on Earth that you feel compelled to solve. When you encounter this problem, something within you stirs, and you think, "Not on my watch!"

Finally, there's the **Why**. When you embrace who you are and find a problem that deeply inspires you, it's time to be the solution. That is your *why*. You'll sense a rising passion and a compelling drive to keep going.

Many of us have been living our purpose without fully realizing it. Discovering your purpose doesn't necessarily require striving. It's about connecting the dots in your life journey and identifying, affirming, and acting upon specific puzzle pieces.

Looking back, I didn't know what I was doing as a

10-year-old. But with over 25 years of experience, research, and serving leaders worldwide, I now have the language to describe what was happening. I must admit, though, that I didn't fully know who I was or why I was here on Earth. That's why I want to highlight the importance of core values and how they helped me become my inner north star.

Behind the Green Apron: In Depth with the Former Starbucks President

The first guest I had on the *Inside Out Leadership* podcast was Howard Behar, the former founding president of Starbucks International. He played a vital role in propelling Starbucks from 28 regional stores to a global presence with over 15,000 stores worldwide.

During our conversation, Howard stressed how crucial it is to show kindness and really *listen* to others instead of jumping to give solutions right away. He also emphasized the significance of having strong values when it comes to building a successful organization. Howard believes that in order for a company to grow and thrive, it's important to prioritize the personal growth and well-being of individuals within the organization. By focusing on serving individuals and building strong teams, he was able to promote the idea of servant leadership, which played a major role in Starbucks' remarkable growth over the years.

I was particularly intrigued by the mindset or perspective from which he served others through active listening—a crucial aspect of receiving.

Howard went on to acknowledge that tensions exist in the marketplace and within organizations with investors and employees always expecting more. To address these tensions, he said it's important to be clear about our values and mission in life. He highlighted that our values should be consistent across all aspects of life and that it is never too late to change and become the person we want to be. Howard encourages individuals to take time to write down their values and hold themselves accountable to them. That way, they can live a life worth planning for and thinking about.

In this process, it's essential to recognize that your definition of specific values may not match others' definitions. And how we define our values can lead to different outcomes or results as well.

Freakonomics data show that having many books at home—a sign of valuing education—is linked to higher test scores in children (from the Early Childhood Longitudinal Study). However, reading to the child daily doesn't significantly impact test scores. That emphasizes the crucial role of core values such as creating a learning-focused environment in shaping a child's academic success.

Reflecting on my interview with Howard Behar, it became clear that my early basketball journey paralleled the broader lessons of life. Howard demonstrated a willingness to embrace the challenges that accompanied new experiences, including personal growth, new team members, and different cultures. One practical aspect that aided him and others in navigating through these difficult times was the acknowledgment, acceptance, and accountability of personal values. That ignited personal growth and contributed to the success of the business.

Despite my initial intimidation when I encountered Abdul, I was drawn to his unwavering passion that transcended our differences. In my interview with Howard, he emphasized the importance of compassion, listening, and embracing diversity of thought, highlighting that true leadership extends beyond appearances and preconceptions.

I realized that Howard and I had both found ourselves immersed in unfamiliar territories, exposed to new ways of life and unique cultures. And just as Howard encouraged individuals to hold themselves accountable to their values, I had been driven to return to basketball practice, eager to learn, adapt, and overcome the challenges that lay ahead.

Howard Behar focused on understanding the values of his team members, and I prioritized learning about basketball. Because of that, both of us were strongly connected to our values, which allowed us to be open to receiving despite the challenges we faced.

Harnessing Freedom to Foster Authentic Connection

How might you use your freedom to promote freedom in others? In other words, the more you embrace your inner north star, the freer you are to authentically receive from others who are different from you. When you truly are free to know who you are and what you value the most, it should liberate you to learn and receive from others and not be threatened by it.

How many leaders (and individuals) do you know who tightly hold on to their values, expending significant energy in an attempt to impose them on others? Unfortunately, that often leads to frustration and creates a rift between the leader and the team members, causing a major disconnect in their relationship.

Instead, let's focus on building bridges rather than burning them!

Consider embracing your values in a way that promotes freedom, allowing you to better understand and learn from the values of others. As a leader, imagine what it would be like if your vision were centered on helping others discover their own visions! The same principle applies to values. When you truly know and embrace your values, it becomes a wonderful opportunity to learn from the values of others.

Startling Encounter

I was en route to be a featured keynote speaker in Fort Worth, Texas. I arrived at the Philadelphia airport, looking forward to the exciting trip ahead.

After getting through security, I went about my usual travel routine of grabbing a newspaper and some snacks. I found an open seat at the departing gate terminal and settled in, anticipating the boarding of my flight in approximately 45 minutes. At that moment, all you need to understand is that I was completely focused on my job—delivering my Inside Out Leadership principles to a group that was very open to it. I was feeling confident and ready for what was about to happen, until . . .

That's when I heard a man shout, "Hey Robb, I can't believe I'm seeing you here!" The man was about 50 feet away from me and appeared very happy to see me.

Initially, I struggled to recall who he was, but as he approached with open arms for a big hug, I remembered him as a friend from my local church community from several years ago.

After we embraced and expressed gratitude for seeing each other, he shared with me that he was traveling from Philadelphia to Dallas for the memorial service of his eight-month-old niece. He and his family were devastated by the loss and planned to spend a week in the area to mourn.

When he told me this surprising news, I was completely caught off guard because I was so focused on what I was doing. It was a sudden interruption that reminded me of my identity and the values I hold dear. In other words, even though the situation was unexpected and involved someone very different from me and in a very different situation, I was able to adapt quickly and accept the new and spontaneous circumstances, which led me to embrace my friend.

As he shared his story, he explained how he felt that seeing me was a sign from God that he wasn't alone. I listened attentively and expressed empathy and compassion for his loss. As we spoke, both of us shed tears.

As we boarded the plane together, we took a selfie to capture the moment and hugged again before taking our seats. I reflected on our conversation and how meaningful it was to me. At the baggage claim after the plane landed, I saw my friend again and briefly met some of his family members. I gave them all hugs and offered prayers for their difficult time.

Reflecting on this encounter, I realized that I was surprised to see my friend at the airport but not surprised at how I responded. I aim to lead with purpose, authenticity, and compassion, and was able to offer my friend the support he needed in that moment.

A few months later, my friend sent me a touching text expressing gratitude for my compassion, encouragement, and kindness during a time when he needed it most. He thanked me for being a vessel of God's love and helping him navigate that difficult week.

That exchange wasn't about what I did but about who we were together at that moment. It reminded me of the importance of knowing ourselves and operating freely from that place to serve others with compassion and authenticity.

Looking back, I now realize that my values were anchoring me more than I had initially thought on my journey with Abdul. Basketball held immense value for me, and I was deeply passionate about improving and becoming the best basketball player I could be. Similarly, Abdul also valued basketball in a profound way. He had a strong desire to work with kids like me who shared the same passion for the sport he loved. It's often surprising how there can be a common thread of beliefs and values that connect people who may appear different at first glance. Unfortunately, we tend to focus on the obvious differences, and that holds us back from recognizing the shared values we actually have.

I am truly grateful for the valuable lesson Abdul taught me about embracing my own north star. I am also thankful to Howard Behar for reinforcing that lesson through our conversation. And I am grateful for the encounter with my friend at the airport. It served as a reminder that we all have more in common than we realize.

Lesson #2

Embrace Your Inner North Star, and Foster a Culture of Connection

When we truly know our true self and embrace our core values, it should liberate us to spend time with and learn from those who hold different values. It goes beyond merely connecting with others; it involves actively seeking diverse perspectives and experiences in order to broaden our understanding and deepen our personal growth. By embracing the richness of diversity, we can expand our horizons, challenge our assumptions, and foster a greater sense of empathy and acceptance.

4 Key Takeaways

1. By placing ourselves in a position to receive from those who are different from us, we discover that our core values serve as our anchor and inner north star.

2. Embracing our true selves with a spirit of exploration opens the door to deeper, more authentic relationships that surpass our wildest imaginations.

3. When you are truly free to know who you are and what you value most, it should liberate you to learn and receive from others and not be threatened by it.

4. It is through this journey of connection and self-discovery that we unlock the transformative power of embracing diversity and forge meaningful connections with others.

Reflection

- Are you aware of your top five personal core values? These are the deep convictions of the heart that guide your decisions each day.

- Have you ever been given a fun nickname? If yes, what was it? If not, what nickname would you choose for yourself and why?

- What is one specific action you are willing to commit to in the next 30 days that will make a tangible difference in fostering your learning from someone who is significantly different from you?

CHAPTER 3

Create Limitless Horizons

*In a perfect healthy spirit gaining a vision
of life and one's fellow men (and women)
and a tree and deep knowledge of nature,
kindness is the natural thing.*

—Abdul

Picture nine people crammed into a 1980s station wagon
driving 45 minutes away to a big basketball tournament.
The nerves of anticipation were so thick you could cut
through it with a knife. Usually one and, to be honest,
sometimes two of us forgot to use deodorant, which
made the body odor get worse as time went on. White,
Hispanic, and African-American, we all came together
in the car, united by one common purpose—to win the
weekend tournament!

Not long after we started the ride, we channeled our

nerves into sharing funny stories and jokes. They made me laugh so much that my sides hurt and my cheeks ached. Yet in the center of it all was one person—Abdul.

Perhaps it was because over half of the people in the car were from Abdul's neighborhood, and they knew him far better than I did. I remember that every story seemed to revolve around Abdul, teasing him about his dating interests, his long hair, and even his time in Vietnam.

Abdul stuck up for himself, raising his voice in the car. He answered questions, questioned what others said, and made our already passionate talks even more lively. We gave him a really hard time, but he was always a good sport, although there were moments when he definitely dished out his fair share.

I remember a particular instance when the guys who knew Abdul best questioned him about a woman they believed had a crush on him. Abdul quickly said they were wrong, but they kept insisting that she liked him. In the end, Abdul was cool about it, handling the teasing and trash talking in a playful way.

All this happened before we reached the tournament. When we got there and were waiting for the first game to start, I couldn't believe how big and strong the other team looked as they warmed up. They were a lot bigger, more powerful, and seemed more organized than our team. And to top it off, they had around 15 players wearing really expensive uniforms!

On the contrary, we showed up with only seven players, some with missing uniform tops, and we looked significantly smaller. We were a diverse bunch, hailing from various walks of life and led by none other than Abdul.

If the warm-ups weren't humbling enough, it didn't take long for us to find ourselves trailing 15 to 4 in the first quarter. Abdul was on the sidelines with his infamous stat chart, urging us to focus on the fundamentals and yelling instructions at us to get in the right place, do the right thing, and make the right moves.

Strangely enough, it seemed that the harder we tried, the worse the score became. As the game unfolded, the score was something like 46 to 11 at halftime.

We felt dejected, not to mention utterly exhausted from being undermanned and undersized. During halftime, Abdul delivered his pep talk, meticulously going over our plays and emphasizing the importance of doing things the right way.

But wouldn't you know it, the second half mirrored the first, and when it was all over, all seven of us were slumped with our heads down, drained, and humiliated. Abdul was the only person with his head held high.

"We can't dwell on feeling down. It's game time for #2!" Abdul shouted. And then a similar situation unfolded in the next game.

Abdul fearlessly devoted himself to teaching us something far more important than winning, which I'll explain in a little bit.

As we piled back into the car—all seven players, my dad, and Abdul—for the 45-minute journey home, Abdul share with us that the team we just played was two grades ahead of us. Talk about perspective! After what we had experienced, I guess it shouldn't have come as too much of a shock.

It didn't take long for us wild kids to shift our focus from basketball back to Abdul and having fun with him. About 15 minutes into the trip home, we stopped at a local convenience store and stocked up on food and drinks for everyone. To my complete surprise, Abdul placed a box of donuts and a soda on the counter, and my dad graciously covered the cost. Later I found out this was one of Abdul's most substantial "meals" of the day!

With nine people crammed in the car and seven of us having played the majority of the game, the stench of body odor was much worse than it was before. In addition, the heat in the car fogged up all the car windows. We cracked open all the windows, desperate for some much-needed fresh air.

In a peculiar way, the car felt like home to me.

We eventually stopped at various homes to drop off two or three players at a time until only Abdul remained in the car with my dad and me. As my dad and I said goodbye to Abdul, we knew that round two of the tournament games was just a few hours away—and probably a similar experience awaited us.

But despite the challenging games, the exhaustion, and the defeats, there was something about Abdul's unwavering spirit that inspired the team. He taught us more than just basketball skills. He instilled in us resilience, camaraderie, and the importance of finding joy on the journey.

The car rides with Abdul were never dull. We shared laughter, stories, and a sense of belonging that transcended our differences. Abdul's ability to bring people together and create a lively atmosphere even in the face of defeat was truly remarkable.

As we embarked on the next day's tournament games, I couldn't help but feel grateful for the opportunity to be part of Abdul's team. We didn't win every game, but the memories we made, the friendships we built, and the powerful lesson of expanding our horizons will stay with us forever.

As I reflect on that time with Abdul, I recognize that the **true victory isn't found in the number of wins but in the profound impact our team spirit had on our growth, resilience, and ability to dream even bigger.**

Amy Watts' article "17 Statistics Unveiling the Significance of Workplace Diversity and Inclusion" highlights the importance of diversity and inclusion. Key statistics include:

1.   Inclusive companies are 1.7 times more likely to be innovation leaders.

2.   Companies with high racial diversity experience a 15-fold increase in sales revenue.

3.   Inclusive teams make better business decisions twice as fast.

4.   Diverse companies are 70% more likely to capture new markets.

5.   Over 75% of job seekers prioritize diversity when considering job offers.

When you intentionally connect with people who are different from you, your horizons naturally expand. As I explained in the previous chapter ("Embrace Your Inner North Star"), knowing your true self and your core values provides a strong foundation that allows you to learn from and be open to those who have different perspectives. It empowers you to envision boundless possibilities without feeling threatened by them or the people who support you on your journey.

Daughter of a Diplomat

In one of the early episodes of the *Inside Out Leadership* Podcast, I had the extraordinary opportunity to sit down with Serena Sumanop, a true visionary and global philanthropist who has transformed the world with her remarkable accomplishments.

Growing up in a family with a diplomat father, Serena had the incredible privilege of traveling and experiencing diverse cultures at a young age. It opened her eyes to a world beyond the boundaries of her own geographical location. While technology has made our world smaller, she believes that being born in the 1980s was advantageous since she witnessed the transformation from large television sets to having TV in the palm of your hand.

Coming from the small island country of Papua, New Guinea (with a population of only 10 million), Serena's father was among the few who received a university education during a time of independence. Riding the wave of liberation from the colonial government, he joined the Foreign Service in the 1980s, which allowed Serena to live in a variety of places. Spending her formative years in Brussels and Tokyo, she attended an exceptional school and interacted with people from diverse cultures. These experiences shaped her perspectives and expectations of the world, instilling in her the importance of education and hard work.

By immersing herself in different cultures, Serena gained a broader perspective and a deeper understanding of the world. This exposure allowed her to witness diverse ways of thinking, living, and approaching life's challenges. Through these interactions, Serena learned the value of openness and receptiveness to new ideas, beliefs, and perspectives. She realizes that there is much to learn from others and that receiving wisdom, knowledge, and experiences from different cultures can deepen her own personal growth and expand her horizons.

In addition, Serena's encounters with people from diverse backgrounds fostered a sense of empathy and compassion in her. By engaging with individuals who have different life stories, struggles, and triumphs, she has developed a deep appreciation for the human experience in all its variations. This empathy allows her to connect with others on a deeper level, understand their perspectives, and build meaningful relationships.

Serena learned the importance of receiving support, guidance, and inspiration from others, recognizing that the strength of her dreams can be amplified through collaboration and shared experiences.

Serena's exposure to different cultures and their unique

approaches to life encourages her to dream big. Witnessing the diversity of human achievements and aspirations fuels her own imagination and ambition. She realizes that there are countless paths to success and fulfillment, and she is inspired to think beyond the confines of her own cultural background. Her interactions with individuals who have pursued their dreams in unconventional ways instill in her the belief that she, too, can aim for greatness, regardless of societal expectations or limitations.

Similar to the car rides with Abdul and the others who were different from me, Serena's interactions with various cultures play a role in her capacity to learn how to accept others and dream big dreams. These experiences, both for Serena and me, show how important it is to be open-minded, understanding, and willing to learn from others' insights and experiences. They have also sparked our creativity and inspired us to chase after our dreams with courage, finding inspiration in the diverse individuals we've encountered along the way.

However, the courage needed on this journey of limitless horizons is most powerfully experienced when you have someone by your side who shares in those big dreams.

Needed Time Away

It had been far too long since my wife, Karen, and I had an overnight getaway together. Between juggling three lively children and dealing with the challenges of

COVID-19 for nearly three years, finding time for ourselves felt like a distant memory. But we knew we needed to prioritize our relationship and make time for each other. So we finally planned a much-needed escape to a cozy bed and breakfast.

We approached this time with open hearts and minds, not knowing exactly what to expect but with a deep sense of excitement and hope. During our 24 hours away, we did some simple yet meaningful things such as a leisurely dinner, a peaceful walk, and some quiet time for reading. But what made this experience truly special was the opportunity to focus on each other and dream big.

Later that night, we went for a walk and found two chairs in a softly lit spot. Something you might not be aware of is that Karen and I enjoy sitting on our front porch or back deck and having conversations. This felt like a familiar scene in a new location, making it seem just perfect. As we talked and shared our thoughts and hopes, something magical began to happen. Our dreams grew bigger, more authentic, and more tangible. And it was all thanks to the power of shared vision. When we take the time to truly connect with those around us, to be present in the moment and focus on each other, the path to our future becomes clearer. We become better stewards of our dreams, committing to doing the right things in the right way.

Karen and I returned home feeling rejuvenated and reconnected with a renewed sense of purpose. We had a shared bond and vision for the future that we were excited to pursue together. And it all started with taking the time to prioritize our relationship and be present with each other.

And now let's return to the story of Abdul. A diverse group of individuals came together with a common purpose—to win a basketball tournament. Through our shared experiences, Abdul taught us resilience, camaraderie, and the importance of finding joy on the journey. The car rides with Abdul were filled with laughter, stories, and a sense of belonging that transcended our differences.

Abdul's unwavering spirit inspired our team, instilling valuable life lessons beyond basketball skills. While we may not have won every game, the memories, bonds, and lessons learned were invaluable. Our collective spirit had a profound impact on our growth, resilience, and ability to dream even bigger.

Abdul's story exemplifies the significance of workplace diversity and inclusion as emphasized in Amy Watts' article. Like Abdul, who fostered unity and vitality even in the midst of defeat, purposefully connecting with people of diverse backgrounds naturally broadens our perspectives. This vital lesson is mirrored in Serena's life and reaffirmed in my own experiences, highlighting the importance of sharing our dreams with someone who supports us wholeheartedly.

Lesson #3

Create Limitless Horizons through Shared Experiences

Whether it's on the basketball court or in the workplace, embracing diversity and fostering inclusion not only enhances innovation, revenue, and decision-making but also creates an environment where individuals can thrive, learn from one another, and dream big dreams. This is most fulfilling when you have someone by your side who shares in your grand aspirations and dreams.

3 Key Takeaways

1.   True victory lies not merely in the number of wins but in the profound impact team spirit has on the ability to dream even bigger.

2.   The strength of our dreams can be amplified through shared experiences.

3.   When we prioritize our relationships and intentionally make time for each other, a beautiful opportunity arises—the chance to dream together.

Reflection

- What was something you pursued without a clear vision or belief in its outcome? What were the eventual results of your pursuit?

- On the other hand, have you ever pursued something with a limitless horizon? What were the eventual outcomes or results of that pursuit?

- Identify a team member who possesses boundless aspirations despite their differences from you. Reach out to them, and schedule a time to discuss and share your mutual aspirations.

CHAPTER 4

Soar Beyond Self

We should lead a decent human life simply because we are decent human beings.

—*Abdul*

Watching Abdul coach was quite an experience.

I recently encountered a friend who shared his perspective on Abdul. He considered Abdul not the greatest x's and o's coach but an exceptional teacher. It's evident that Abdul's leadership approach was distinct and transformative, resonating with those who were open to embrace it.

I couldn't help but be blown away by Abdul with his clipboard in hand, meticulously taking down every statistic for every player on our team. Not only was he tracking points, offensive rebounds, defensive rebounds, steals, block shots, assists, free throws made, free throws missed, and field goal attempts, he was also calling out plays, providing much-needed corrections, and even offering occasional applause. It was all happening in such a seamless way that I couldn't help but wonder how he managed to do it all. He was doing it for everyone on the entire team.

But there was a method to his madness.

As any effective coach knows, keeping accurate records of each team member's performance is essential for improvement throughout the season. And that was exactly what Abdul was doing—making sure each player was given the necessary instruction to reach their full potential.

But what really stood out to me was Abdul's obsession with doing the right thing rather than just obsessing over winning. Even when we were down by 20 points and seemingly didn't care about the score, Abdul remained focused on helping us improve as individual players and as a team. He knew that winning would eventually be a natural byproduct of doing things the right way.

As I mentioned in the previous chapter, we lost far more games than we won. Being the competitor that I am, that drove me up the wall with frustration. But as I reflect back on that experience, I realize that Abdul's approach to coaching was far more valuable than any win or championship could have ever been.

Abdul dedicated himself to helping me grasp the intricacies of the game. But he also encouraged relentless practice, aiming for a place of excellence that would make me embody the very essence of the game. I'll explain the reasons behind his unusual approach using real-life examples in Chapter 6.

As I started my journey with Abdul at the age of 10, I gradually began to grasp and appreciate his goals, especially as I entered my early teens. Just like many aspects of life, the more we invest in ourselves and see positive changes, the easier it is to stay on the path. Unfortunately, so many leaders (and individuals) don't see immediate outcomes, only to give up way too early. This process causes them to abandon their goals, only to later realize that success was closer than they initially believed. Even better, they might discover that what they aimed for was too small and that something even greater than they could imagine awaited them.

I'm glad I kept going and realized that when you work hard and practice at something, incredible things happen—although not always as I initially expected.

The Music Will Find You

I had the unique and special opportunity to have a con-versation a couple years ago with Michael Gerber, the author of one of my all-time favorite business books. According to *Inc.* magazine, Michael is the "World's #1 Small Business Guru" who has impacted millions of small business owners worldwide for over 40 years. His bestselling *E-Myth* book series, including *The E-Myth Revisited*, offers essential insights into entrepreneurship, leadership, and management, inspiring lasting success in the small business realm.

During our 30-minute conversation, Michael shared about Merle, his transformative mentor who was not only a saxophone perfectionist but also instilled a pro-found life lesson similar to the one Abdul instilled in me. Merle emphasized to Michael that through dedicat-ed practice, the music would find you. Similarly, when you commit to practicing and working on yourself, you will naturally discover your true self. By investing time and effort in personal growth, you embark on a journey of self-discovery, enabling your authentic essence to unfold. Merle's wisdom beautifully resonates with the notion that just as music finds those who diligently prac-tice, true self-awareness and fulfillment come to those who wholeheartedly invest in working on themselves.

This realization hit me the hardest on the night before my first professional basketball tryout. I had received an invitation to the training camp for the Delaware Blue

Bombers, a team in the Atlantic Basketball Association (ABA). My sister called and asked if I was overly nervous about this incredible opportunity. I can still vividly recall my response: "I've been training my entire life for this moment!"

All the hours of practice, meticulous attention to detail, and relentless hard work I had poured into my basketball journey had prepared me for this precise moment. Abdul's and Howard's wisdom rang true, and so did Merle's—the music would indeed find me. I'll share more about the outcome and experiences during the professional basketball tryout in Chapter 7. Stay tuned!

I'm worn out

I'm thinking about a good friend who's a top leader in a growing and influential organization. He's a hard worker, a team player, and really good at leading. But lately, he's been facing far more tough challenges in just a few months than most businesses face in years. It has left him feeling like he's lost his motivation.

After talking to him, I wondered, "How can someone keep pushing forward when they're doing everything they know to do but it seems like there's always something difficult coming their way?"

This is when you must be willing to receive deeply from others in your life and on your team, much like how trees use their roots to connect. In the *New York Times* best-selling book *The Hidden Life of Trees*, author Peter

Wohlleben reveals that trees help one another through their interconnected roots. They grow tiny hairs on these roots to absorb as much water as possible, which they then share with trees of the same species that are in need. They even form partnerships with something very different—fungi—which end up acting like helpful friends. Although they seemingly pose a threat, fungi actually protect the trees and provide valuable resources in exchange for a beneficial substance from the trees.

Similarly, leaders (and all of us) should tap into the support of those around us—friends, family, and team members who genuinely care about our well-being. Their encouragement can be like essential water during times when we feel drained. However, an even more significant form of support may come from an unexpected source.

During my conversation with my friend, I passionately shared that there will be friends, family members, and team members who will jump at the opportunity to offer their support. I said to let yourself absorb that support system by simply allowing them to help you. I know it's sometimes easier said than done. Get ready for the "how to" in Chapter 7.

But then there are those who might not seem interested or don't show much concern. They might even say something like, "Don't worry, you've got this!" but then they don't follow up. It might seem like they're not caring, but there's a possibility you can receive from them in a profound way, even if it's not as obvious as you expect.

Being open to receiving from them in a new way might be exactly what you need. So even if the people around us don't change their behavior, we can change how we perceive them and how we allow them to assist us. This change in perspective can lead us to the inspiration we've been seeking, just like music finds its way to us.

My experience with my mom was somewhat similar to this.

Mom's Christmas Present

It came that time of year when I had to rack my brain to find the perfect Christmas gift for my mom. The challenge was real because, let's face it, she didn't really need much, and over the years, I had already given her just about everything under the sun.

After long conversations with my wife and much contemplation, I pondered whether it was time to go with the usual framed pictures of our grandkids. It's a popular choice for those entering the twilight years. But deep down, I knew I wanted to think outside the box, to surprise her with something truly unique.

And that's when my wife came to the rescue. She suggested the idea of a subscription that aligned with my mom's passion—plants with interesting textures. You see, my mom has always had an appreciation for artistic expressions since she is an artist herself.

What's important to understand is that this all unfolded during one of the most challenging periods of my life. I was dealing with some heavy personal issues. My mom has always been an incredible pillar of support and one of the strongest sources of encouragement in my life. However, due to her significant physical limitations, including the burden of neuropathy, she couldn't make as many spontaneous or planned trips to see me like she used to.

In the past, an in-person visit or a lengthy phone call from her was like medicine for my soul, especially during tough times. I was accustomed to receiving her support in a certain way. Now, the situation had changed, not because she cared any less but because her physical condition restricted her options. I had to adjust my expectations and find a new way to connect with her, one that worked within her limitations while still providing the support I needed.

As I finalized the details of the plant subscription, a brilliant idea dawned on me. Those ideas don't come too often, so I had to take full advantage of this moment. Why not arrange for the plants to be delivered to my doorstep every month for a span of six months? That way, I could personally deliver each plant to my mom, spending precious quality time with her. That's her love language, or some may call it the language of appreciation.

This simple act of intentionally doing something for her allowed me to meet her on her own terms and enabled me to not only give but also receive her presence in a way that was different from what I was used to. You see, spending quality time with people is one of my mom's greatest gifts, and this gift of plant deliveries would keep on giving, at least for half a year. But it wasn't just about the physical gift; it was about setting up a scenario where I could connect with my mom where she was and receive from her in a new and meaningful way.

Before I knew it, the first plant arrived at my door. I looked forward to the moment I could hand it over to my mom, knowing that this simple act would build a deeper connection between us.

Alright, you might be wondering how all of this ties into the idea of "soaring beyond self." Well, here's the connection. When you commit to staying on the path of pursuing excellence, which in my book means giving your absolute best with the resources you've got, there's a beautiful reward waiting for you down the line. But let's be real. It's not a smooth ride. Along the way, you're going to face challenges, tough times, and obstacles that might feel like they're holding you back.

This is where the magic happens. In those moments of difficulty, you must deliberately open yourself up to receive support from the people around you—friends, family, those who aren't like you. These are the unexpected allies who can provide the boost you need to push through, to keep that forward momentum.

When you embrace this idea of receiving support, even from unexpected sources, you begin to transcend your own limitations. You start to achieve things that might have seemed impossible before. This is how we rise above our own selves and our own doubts and achieve greatness. So the key takeaway is this: as you pursue excellence, stay open to the support that comes your way, even if it's from places you didn't anticipate. That is how you soar beyond yourself and accomplish things that once seemed out of reach.

Proven Impact on Our Lives (and the Lives of Others)

There's a research study by Dr. Grant Hilary Brenner about going beyond ourselves. He looked closely at people's life stories to find out what makes them push past their limits. The study found six important things that help us do that: finishing things, feeling connected to others, always learning, having strong relationships, reaching our full potential, and respecting different spiritual beliefs.

By listening to people's stories, the study showed that these factors play a big role in helping us move beyond just thinking about ourselves. It's about closing chapters, being connected, growing, having good relationships, reaching our best, and respecting different ways people believe.

These findings offer valuable insights into the essence of what Abdul wanted me to discover. They shed light on the core principles and aspects that Abdul wanted me to experience firsthand.

Lesson #4

Soar beyond Self to Transform Self

When you're willing to receive help, even from surprising places, you can go beyond what you thought was possible. That is how you overcome your own limits and doubts, and reach greatness. The main idea is this: as you aim for excellence, be open to the support that comes your way, even if it's unexpected. This openness is how you surpass yourself and achieve things that once felt impossible.

4 Key Takeaways

1.   Aim for excellence in whatever you do.

2.   You will reap a reward if you don't give up.

3.   Leverage your wide-ranging connections with both the familiar and the unfamiliar in order to seek assistance in overcoming obstacles.

4.   When you understand that the world is much big-

ger than just you, you'll start to feel a natural sense of growth inside you.

Reflection

- Imagine something you really love doing such as a hobby, job, or something you're interested in. Think about how you put your whole heart into it, spending a lot of time and effort while practicing and getting better over a good amount of time. Now, look at what happened because you worked so hard at it. How did you feel inside? What changed about you because of this?

- Can you think of a time in your life when you received support or help from an unexpected source? How did that experience shape your perspective of your own capabilities and what you thought was achievable?

Part II

Courage Sustains Significance

CHAPTER 5

Core Resilience Rises

*The enjoyment of life covers many things:
the enjoyment of ourselves, home life,
trees, flowers, clouds, winding rivers and
the myriad of things in nature, and then the
enjoyment of poetry, art, contemplation,
friendship, conversation, and reading.*

—Abdul

I remember like it was yesterday when Abdul came over to my house for meals. Whenever vegetables were passed his way, the look on his face was priceless. It was as if he couldn't believe someone would offer him something so healthy. His immediate response was, "Why do I need that?" He quickly followed that with a firm, "I don't eat those." We often suggested, "It might be good for you to add some fruits and veggies to your diet," but I don't remember a time when he ever took us up on that. Of course, when it came to meat and potatoes, Abdul couldn't say yes fast enough.

Abdul didn't typically visit our house alone. Since he couldn't drive, we picked him up and then took him back home after the meal. But usually, one of his former players picked him up and came with him, and we all enjoyed a meal together. That usually happened a few times per year, mostly during holidays such as Christmas, Thanksgiving, and Easter.

As soon as Abdul arrived, the focus shifted entirely to him. Of course, it's not unusual in American culture to give guests some attention, but Abdul absorbed it all in a very unique way. He had a presence that drew everyone in, and the attention he received over the next few hours was far more than the average guest.

We never had a problem with that, even though my siblings and I always craved attention. We liked it because when we gave Abdul attention, he made sure there was enough attention to go around. My parents often facilitated the conversation, and if it ever got too out of hand with crazy stories or too much poking fun, they reeled us in.

That happened more times than I'd like to admit.

I remember a story Abdul told us about baking during the Vietnam War. Yes, he was indeed a baker during the war! He got us so curious that he promised to make us his most popular treat from that time—cinnamon rolls.

At first, we didn't take him seriously and thought he was just kidding. But within a few weeks, he surprised us with cinnamon rolls that tasted more like dinner rolls. He handed them to us in a brown grocery bag. The oil had soaked through the bottom of the bag.

When it came time to eat, we all took our seats, said a prayer, and started passing the food that my mom had spent the last few hours making. Despite Abdul's distaste for vegetables and his love for meat and potatoes, what I remember most about our meals wasn't what he ate or didn't eat but rather the laughter and stories we shared. Abdul was a man who was much different than we were, but we loved to make fun of him and hear his quick comebacks. In some ways, I was far more curious about him than I realized. I wanted to learn, understand, and know what made him tick.

Inviting Abdul for meals became a wonderful way to build a stronger connection and deepen our relationship with him. He had his own story, and over time, I was gradually getting to know both the story and the person behind it. Just think what I would have missed out on if I had limited our interaction only to the basketball court or those infamous car rides.

A study from 2017 at the University of Oxford found that when people eat together more often, they're more likely to feel connected to others and happy with their lives. Professor Robin Dunbar from the Experimental Psychology Department at the University of Oxford said, "This study shows that eating together is really important for bringing people closer, and it's possible that humans developed communal eating as a way to help us bond with each other."

I am extremely thankful to my parents for regularly inviting Abdul over to our house so we could learn from him and get to know him. Everyone has a story, and when we spend extended time with them during shared meals, we not only value their background but also incorporate their journey as meaningful aspects of our own.

Get in the C.A.R.

I had the privilege of talking with Monte Williams, a TEDx speaker and the founder of ALEU. A few years ago, he delivered a famous TEDx talk called "Get in the C.A.R. – The Keys to Sustainable Leadership." During our conversation, a pivotal moment from Monte's life captured my attention. It showcased the power of hearing someone's story over a meal or through a spontaneous interaction.

Monte shared a milestone from his childhood when he was around 10 years old. His parents had gone through a divorce, and his mother who was battling mental health issues was really struggling. One day, Monte failed to provide a satisfactory answer to a question his mother asked, and in a fit of frustration, she kicked Monte out of the house with a note in his pocket that read, "I want to know."

Looking for a place to spend the night, Monte found himself in a local park where something unusual happened. A homeless man crossed his path, and unexpectedly, this stranger took Monte under his wing. Over a shared meal, Monte opened up about his struggles. The homeless man empathized, recognizing the weight of the situation.

During their conversation, the homeless man shared with Monte two profound truths. He acknowledged that this would be the toughest day of Monte's life, but if he woke up to see the morning sun, he would have the resilience to face any challenge life threw his way.

That night, tears streaming down his face, Monte cried himself to sleep. But when he woke up, he experienced something beautiful—the warm sun shining on his face. At that moment, Monte said to himself, "You made it. You made it through the night." It dawned on him that the homeless man provided the courage he needed to press on.

This story exemplifies the immense power of hearing someone's story over a meal or through a spontaneous interaction. **In those vulnerable and unexpected moments, societal boundaries dissolve, and connections are formed.** Whether it is sharing a meal or engaging in an unplanned conversation, these encounters create a safe space for stories to unfold, pain to be shared, and seeds of empathy, compassion, and resilience to be planted.

In her insightful article titled "What Makes Storytelling So Effective for Learning?" Vanessa Boris delves into the reasons behind the remarkable effectiveness of storytelling as a tool for learning.

Stories have the ability to forge connections among people and ideas, conveying the shared culture, history, and values that bind us together. This is true not only in our personal lives but also in the business world.

Stories go beyond creating a sense of connection; they also build familiarity, trust, and openness to learning. A good story allows the listener to enter the narrative from their own perspective, making them more receptive to new ideas. Stories can also convey multiple meanings, making complex concepts more accessible and memorable. They are far more engaging than simply presenting data or discussing abstract ideas.

To illustrate the power of storytelling, Boris presents a scenario where two companies hold meetings to discuss their quarterly results. In Company A, the leader presents the financial numbers, while in Company B, the leader tells a captivating story about the strategy that led to their success. The employees in Company A walk away with the knowledge that they met their targets, but the employees in Company B learn about an effective strategy that brought together various departments to secure a major deal. The story leaves them with new knowledge and perspectives, influencing their thinking and facilitating their learning.

In essence, storytelling has a unique ability to connect, engage, and educate. It is a tool that leaders can use to learn from each other, share important information, and inspire their teams. By leveraging the power of storytelling, leaders (and all people) can create meaningful and impactful learning experiences.

RJ's Ambulance Trip

A short time ago, my family went through a deeply challenging experience involving my aunt's passing. I had the privilege of officiating at her memorial service, which became a time of deep reflection, meaning, and celebration of her life. Following the service, our family and close friends gathered at a local restaurant to continue honoring her memory. Picture a buffet-style arrangement with a diverse group of people coming together. We joined tables, creating an intimate atmosphere—a time of comfort and support as we navigated the grieving process together.

However, in the middle of our time together, something blindsided us. My attention was suddenly drawn to my wife who was urgently signaling to me. It turned out that my 13-year-old son was experiencing a major problem. And when it comes to my oldest son, any issue immediately grabs our attention. You see, he has dealt with a severe nut allergy, particularly peanuts, since he was very young. It has become second nature for us to carry an EpiPen wherever we go, just in case.

In this particular moment, his mouth was burning. And when his mouth burns, it triggers our concern. The situation worsened as he developed increased hives inside his mouth, and his throat began to close up. It felt as if someone had a grip around his neck, making it increasingly difficult for him to breathe. Panic, fear, and anxiety closed in on us.

Have you ever experienced such a situation where challenges and trials seem to converge on you or a loved one? The harder you try to regain control, the more it slips from your grasp. That was precisely how we felt.

At that moment, the look on my wife's face said it all. It was clear that our initial plan of administering Benadryl wouldn't suffice. We needed to take swift action with the EpiPen. She motioned for me to step aside, away from the crowd of people, even our intimate family members. The three of us—my wife, my 13-year-old son, and I—quickly walked to the hallway. There, my wife grabbed the EpiPen and took off its protective cap. Holding my son in my arms, she swung her arm and administered it through his clothes, directly into his thigh. In response, my son shouted, "Ow!" She then proceeded to rub his leg while I carefully lowered my son to the ground, supporting my boy.

It's important to note that whenever the EpiPen is used, it is crucial to immediately call 911. If the EpiPen fails to take effect, precious minutes are wasted, potentially endangering his life. Thankfully, with the combined power of the EpiPen and the prayers of our family, the tension and constriction around his throat eased. However, the ambulance was already on its way. When it arrived, the EMTs assessed his vital signs. While his vitals seemed stable, there was still a significant enough reaction that prompted their decision to transport him to the emergency room. They asked, "Who wants to accompany him?" My wife and I exchanged glances, and I suggested that she go while I stayed with our other two children and the rest of the family.

What seemed like a matter of seconds (in reality a couple of minutes), she quickly hopped into the ambulance with RJ, and they sped off to the hospital. I stayed in touch with my wife through text messages, learning about the ongoing situation. An hour passed and then two, and eventually, four hours went by. RJ now began vomiting violently as his body reacted to the allergens unknowingly ingested during the meal. Finally, after a grueling five hours at the emergency room, the medical staff said he was ready to be released. With my other two children by my side, we eagerly picked up my wife and our resilient 13-year-old son. The ordeal had come to an end, and he was going to be okay.

If you've ever encountered a moment where the life of someone you deeply care about hangs in the balance and you find yourself doing everything in your power but feeling utterly helpless, it shakes you to your core. Whether it's an extreme circumstance like ours or a less intense situation but one that still rattles you, you understand the depth of vulnerability that can emerge.

Don't you know that the same vulnerability is present when we allow ourselves to receive from people who are different from us? It makes us feel weak, out of control, and helpless.

You Are More Courageous Than You Think

For my family and me, this experience was eye-opening. It made us realize the depth of love we have for our son. It sparked a desire to support him and our family in ways that are hard to put into words. And I also felt the need to extend that love to those in my circle of influence.

It was like getting to know Abdul and like Monte's experience with the homeless man. They had an impact on me. The same can happen to you when you learn from those who are different. Opening yourself up to learning from others who aren't like you might make you feel vulnerable. However, as you spend time getting to know them, you can also experience a powerful awakening.

Lesson #5

Core Resilience Rises

When we embrace our own stories and actively listen to the stories of others, we cultivate understanding and empathy. Sharing meals and engaging in spontaneous conversations provide powerful avenues for connecting hearts and building a stronger core together. It is through these interactions that we have the opportunity to receive from others such as Abdul and truly understand their perspectives. By opening ourselves up to receive from others in a genuine way, it requires vulnerability to foster deeper connections and enrich our own growth in the process.

4 Key Takeaways

1. The power of storytelling: Storytelling has a unique ability to forge connections among people and ideas. It conveys culture, history, and values, creating a sense of unity and understanding.

2. Building empathy: Engaging in conversations and sharing meals can foster empathy. By actively listening to the stories of others, we gain a deeper understanding of their experiences, perspectives, and emotions.

3. Authentic connection: Genuine and spontaneous interactions create an environment for authentic connections to thrive. These connections go beyond surface-level conversations and build trust, familiarity, and openness to learning.

4. Strengthening relationships: Sharing meals and engaging in spontaneous conversations can strengthen relationships. These moments provide opportunities to connect on a deeper level, share laughter, and build stronger bonds with those around us.

Reflection

- When was the last time you intentionally spent time with someone, not to give but solely to receive and learn from them? Who was the person you were with, and what specific insights or lessons did you gain from that experience?

- Do you consider yourself skilled at asking thought-provoking questions? If so, what is the go-to question you ask someone to encourage them to share a personal story about themselves?

- What is one core belief you have that differs from someone who is important in your life? Are you open to scheduling a meeting with them within the next 30 days to understand their story and perspective better in an effort to learn and gain insight into their specific belief that differs from yours?

CHAPTER 6

Self-Discipline Shapes Outcomes

I do think if you stick by your work, believe in yourself, never give up, and keep saying to yourself, I know I'm good, it'll happen.

—*Abdul*

Just like a scene from the movie *Hoosiers*, Abdul set up folding chairs in a specific way, making a zigzag path. We had to dribble a basketball in a line, first with our left hand and then quickly switch to our right hand as we got closer to the basket. It was super important to get it right. Dribbling with the wrong hand or turning the wrong way made Abdul step in. He was patient, though, guiding us through every step.

We did it over and over until we nailed it. If we struggled

or messed up, Abdul said, "Hit the floor!" That meant for us to drop down and give him a specific number of fingertip push-ups before we could continue. The number of push-ups depended on how serious the mistake was or how bad our attitudes were toward his correction.

I think my fingers still hurt.

Abdul had another favorite drill that focused on getting rebounds when the other team took a shot. He threw the ball off the backboard, and we had to jump up and catch it in the air. The tricky part was that we couldn't let the ball come down; we had to stay up and use our outer foot as a pivot and then swing outward to look for a teammate to pass it to down the court.

I often got confused about which foot to pivot on. It felt more natural to pivot on the foot that was closer to the middle, but Abdul would yell, "You're going the wrong way!" He quickly showed me the right way, and then we would do it all over again. And again. And again.

I feel like my outside foot for defensive rebounds is still glued to the floor.

Like many kids in their early teen years, the primary goal is to have fun and avoid the hard work that comes with getting better. Trust me, I was no different. This mindset often led to negative attitudes, drama, and trouble. Not having any children of his own, Abdul still knew the makeup of kids in this season of life and reinforced many good values. He established clear boundaries and consequences, and made sure everyone understood his expectations.

Even when we faced consequences, Abdul had a special knack for making them into important lessons. He knew we could learn important things when things didn't go well and that we could get better through tough situations. Instead of just giving us regular consequences for mistakes, he had us do unusual things such as fingertip push-ups that we'd even laugh about in the moment.

Abdul taught us that it's like a song you repeat over and over until you know it by heart. We talked about this in Chapter 4 (when the music finds you). But the main thing Abdul wanted us to understand was the value of *self-discipline*. No matter how much we felt like doing it, he said it was important to practice the fundamentals as much as possible and do them just right. He knew that if we kept working hard, it would pay off in the end. At first, I was just looking for fun, but in time I started to embrace what he was talking about. Abdul knew something I didn't, that if I consistently worked hard and paid close attention to the little things, it would set me up to do well in the future.

At the end of practice, we always played a game I loved called "slap back." It was so much fun! In the game, there was a line right under the basket. Each player took a turn throwing the ball out to the free-throw line. As soon as they threw it, they became the defender who was trying to stop the other player's shot. The rules were simple. The person with the ball couldn't dribble or move; they had to shoot right away. If they scored, they kept being the one with the ball. But if they missed, the roles switched. The goal was to see who could make the most shots in a row. It was exciting and made us compete with each other.

When I first started playing the game, my shots always got blocked. But Abdul taught me the trick to success— shoot the ball quickly, and make it go high in the air. I can still hear him telling me, "Greyhound, you've got to shoot like this!" I'll explain more about why he called me Greyhound later in the book.

Suffering Is Optional

In a really interesting interview with my friend Cy Wakeman, a *New York Times* best-selling author and drama researcher, Cy talked about her life and what she's learned about the power of choice.

Cy grew up in a family of business owners, and she had a lot of tough times. She learned how to put her own needs aside and keep things peaceful. But even in the middle of all that, she realized something important—that we can *choose* to be happy and kind, even when things are hard. Cy had her own problems to deal with. Her parents got divorced when she was in high school, which was really tough. But she found ways to feel free and better, and she saw how much change can help.

Looking back on her life, Cy talked about how important it is to become a better leader by working on ourselves. She said we should understand where we come from, think about how our early experiences affect us, and see how they shape what we do and believe. By looking at our past and thinking about our stories, we can learn things that help us become better leaders.

While listening to Cy's amazing words, her story reminded me that no matter how big our problems, we can decide to be happy and fulfilled. That means we need to be really good at making choices and having discipline so our way of thinking matches how we want to feel. I learned this from Abdul, who showed me how important choices and discipline are.

Watching Abdul during practices made me realize I can always choose what to do. I can either stay focused on my goals and be disciplined, or I can go for things that give me quick happiness but don't last long. Abdul's strong dedication to his work taught me that we don't have to suffer if we don't want to. We have control over how we feel by the choices we make and how we think.

Abdul's teachings were a lot like what Cy said. They showed me that growing as a person is really important. Both of their stories came together for me, reminding me how powerful discipline and making smart choices can be. If we use discipline and pick things that match what we care about and want, we can have a good life full of happiness and meaning.

People like Abdul and Cy have taught me that real happiness isn't just something you reach someday. It's how you live your life. To make that happen, we have to be good at making choices and having discipline. We need to face problems and choose to get better instead of staying the same. Thinking about their wisdom makes me want to use the power of choice and discipline in my own journey of learning about myself and growing as a person.

Self-Discipline = Happiness

Being in control of yourself leads to feeling happy. An article called "Yes, but Are They Happy? Effects of Trait Self-Control on Affective Well-Being and Life Satisfaction" by Wilhelm Hofmann and other researchers looked at how being good at controlling ourselves affects how we feel and how satisfied we are with our lives. They conducted three studies with different groups of people and found that when people are better at self-control, they tend to feel better and are more satisfied with their lives. Being able to handle challenges and goals well was a big part of why that happens. The study also showed that self-control helps people not feel too stressed and keeps them balanced when they're working toward their goals.

How to Enhance Your Self-Discipline

1. *Intentional and consistent self-care is a must.*

In my first book, *Lead the Way: Inside Out Leadership Principles for Business Owners & Leaders*, I devote an entire chapter on how you can lead yourself first.

We are three-part beings comprised of spirit, soul, and body. To lead ourselves effectively, we must prioritize self-care in all three areas.

Let's start with the spiritual aspect, which goes beyond words and taps into our purpose and deepest place of who we are. I personally nurture my spiritual connection through daily gratitude, prayer, and worship. How do you nurture your spiritual self?

Moving on to the soul, which encompasses our mind, will, emotions, and imagination, we must engage in activities that feed and refresh us. Talking deeply with friends and family and reading thought-provoking books help me grow. What things or experiences light up your soul?

Finally, our bodies require regular maintenance, just like any moving part. A healthy diet, proper hydration, and consistent exercise are essential. Find physical activities you enjoy, and commit to them. I've found that playing basketball and sticking to a regular exercise plan with weightlifting and running are really important to me.

Most physiologists agree that doing the following on a weekly basis is the minimum our bodies require for health and longevity:

- At least five days aerobic exercise for a duration of at least 30 minutes. Power walking is one of the best ways to satisfy that requirement.

- Two days of some form of weight training. The burpee with integrated push-ups is the best single load-bearing exercise you can do.

- One day of rest.

- I'd like to delve further into the concept of rest for a moment.

It's worth noting that elite athletes, including Olympians, place equal importance on their rest days as they do on their training days. In a 2018 article by Georgina Berbari titled "Why Olympic Athletes' Rest Days Are Just as Important as Their Training Sessions," she explains how many Olympic athletes opt for active rest days instead of completely taking a day off. During these active rest days, the goal is to allow muscles to repair and restore by engaging in low-intensity workouts that facilitate muscle recovery without straining them excessively.

Let's not overlook the significance of quality sleep. Aim for at least seven hours of sleep each night to support your overall well-being. Remember, neglecting any aspect of our being can have an impact on other areas of our lives. In relation to sleep, Berbari emphasizes that many Olympic athletes strictly adhere to getting 8 to 10 hours of sleep each night. Adequate sleep is vital in order for them to perform at their best since it allows their muscles to rest and recover from the rigorous training they undergo daily.

If Olympians value rest, we should too! We are interconnected beings, and it is crucial to prioritize self-care in our spirit, soul, and body in order to thrive holistically. Just as elite athletes understand the value of rest, we, too, can prioritize rest to support our well-being and overall performance in life.

   2. *Set goals.*

In my book *Lead the Way*, the chapter titled "Create a

Plan of Action" delves into the importance of strategic planning. The chapter serves as a roadmap for individuals who are seeking to achieve their goals and make a meaningful impact. Talk about self-discipline!

When you're thinking about your life's plan, it's super important to know exactly what you want and how to make it happen. Let's spend a moment planning the next 12 months and coming up with three good steps to get you started.

First, make a cool mantra for your plan. This is a strong sentence that sums up what you want your whole year to be about. It helps you decide what's important and choose actions. For example, you could use "Be smart, not super busy!" or whatever words mean a lot to you.

Then think about five good things you want to make happen in the next year. Those things should be clear and fit in different parts of your life like family, career, feeling good in your mind, and being healthy. They should be things you're sure about and can think about in a positive way during the year.

For example, one of your things could be spending more time with your family and having stronger, better relationships.

Now let's break down your big goals into smaller steps for each month. Make a plan for three months, and choose one small step for each of your five things. These steps should be clear and doable, and they should help you get closer to your big goals. You should also have someone who can help you stick to your plan and keep going.

For instance, in January, you can plan a fun family outing such as going to the movies. That will bring you closer to your family. In February, you could find a babysitter to watch your kids so you can have a special night with your partner. That's good for your relationship. In March, plan a special hangout with a friend to make your connection stronger.

Do this every three months during the year, and if you need to, change your steps. By planning ahead and doing things on purpose, you'll make a map for being successful and getting better in all parts of your life.

Abdul would feel proud because we're talking about making a plan and doing things ahead of time to strengthen the muscle of self-discipline.

Lesson #6

Self-Discipline Shapes Outcomes

We can control how we feel by the choices we make and how we think. It's really important how much self-control and smart choices can change our lives. If we use discipline and pick things that match what we care about and want, we can move past hard times and have a life that's full of meaning, happiness, and good things.

3 Key Takeaways

1. Regardless of our desire or motivation, Abdul stressed the importance of working on specific skills with dedication and executing them correctly, knowing that disciplined effort would yield long-term rewards.

2. No matter the magnitude of challenges we encounter, we have the power to choose a path of happiness and fulfillment.

3. Intentional and consistent self-care is a must.

Reflection

- What is one intentional decision you are committed to making in order to cultivate stronger self-discipline in your life?

- In which aspect of your life are you finding yourself drawn to the appeal of immediate gratification and fleeting pleasure? What specific steps will you take within the next 48 hours to ensure that you stay on the path of self-discipline?

- Which particular aspect of self-care (body, soul, spirit) are you dedicated to improving? And to ensure accountability and support, who will you share this commitment with?

CHAPTER 7

Silent Strength Radiates

When I look around, I always learn something, and that is to be yourself, to express yourself, and have faith in yourself.

—Abdul

Remember Chapter 4 when I told you my sister called me the night before my first professional tryout? My words rang true! I walked into that training camp with confidence and played some of the best basketball of my life. I made the team and signed my first professional basketball contract in the Atlantic Basketball Association (ABA). My childhood dream had come true!

The first year was limited to the practice team and some spotty regular season minutes due to really good competition. But by the second year, I had proven myself and worked my way to starter and got considerable minutes. That's when I started to invite family members and friends to my games.

I thought there was no better time than now to invite Abdul.

I picked a day for him to come and watch. We both felt more and more excited as it got closer to the day of the game. It was going to be the first time he saw me play in a professional game.

"Good job, Greyhound!" Abdul shouted as I finished signing autographs and made my way through the crowd to where he was. Just so you know, he started calling me Greyhound when I was in my mid-teens after we'd been together for a while. He gave me that nickname because, like the dog, I was skinny and fast.

Although I don't recall much more about our interactions before and after the game, what remains vivid is the impact of his presence. I find it remarkable that a man known for his loud voice and many words had so little to say on the biggest stage I've ever played on.

When I was around Abdul, something powerful took place. Abdul represented the result of all the hard work, self-discipline, and many sacrifices I had made up to that point. His strong belief in what I could do sparked a big change inside me. It wasn't just a feeling of fitting in anymore; it was a strong belief that I had what it takes to make a real difference at the top level. It's one thing to feel like you belong, and it's another thing to know you can contribute at the highest level. I could feel how much he believed in me, and I fully embraced that feeling.

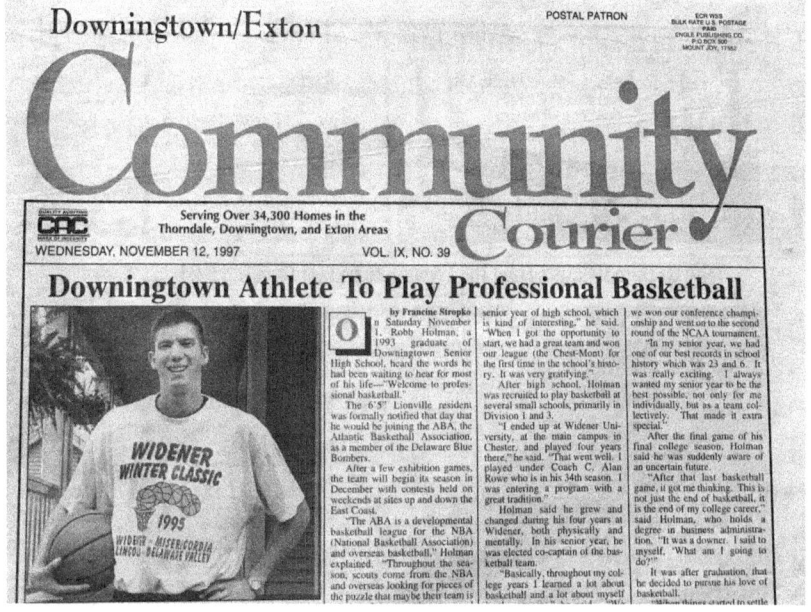

In a weird way, it felt like it was time for me to give what I had received from Abdul.

Thinking about it now, I understand that this is what a mentor does. Mentors do more than what's expected. They support you no matter what, they are always there for you, and they believe in you even when you're not sure of yourself. And if you're willing to receive from them, there will be moments when you can give from a much deeper part of yourself than you could ever have thought possible!

Inviting Abdul to see my game was like giving him an important award, a way for me to say thanks for all his hard work helping me and many others. He also gave me some ideas to get better. After our games, I really looked forward to Abdul saying I did well, but I also listened closely when he talked about where I could improve. His advice was what really made me get better. He knew that no matter how good I played, there was always something more I could learn in order to be my best.

It's interesting to note that Abdul was really great at teaching, even though he wasn't a very good player himself. He wasn't the best at shooting, dribbling, or passing, but he could break down techniques and guide us like no one else. I used to wonder how someone who wasn't so good at playing could be such a good teacher.

The difference between his teaching and playing showed how well he understood the game. He paid attention to all the little details (remember how he recorded lots of stats for different players in Chapter 3) and made everything work together seamlessly. Most importantly, he taught us the core values of the game, not just the basic skills.

But the most amazing thing was how powerful his few words (or even his silence) could be. It inspired me to keep pursuing excellence on and off the basketball court.

The Strength of Support

While talking with Jasmine Romaine, a well-known motivational speaker and best-selling author, her words really hit me. I was captivated by Jasmine's heartfelt tribute to her mother. She talked about how her mother had a big impact on her life. It was really moving. She mentioned her mother's strong faith and the important lessons she taught her. These lessons made her believe strongly in miracles from God, which gave her confidence in herself and fueled her desire to make a positive difference.

Jasmine's mother was a dedicated teacher and showed the importance of giving back, which left a lasting impression on Jasmine's life. Feeling grateful for her own upbringing, Jasmine now supports women, drawing inspiration from her remarkable mother. As we continued talking, we discussed how having a solid foundation from a parent (and a mentor) can be extremely important and how it changes how we see things. Jasmine talked about how her mother's stories and unwavering faith gave her the courage to be bold and confident, despite some childhood insecurities and challenges.

If we were without the unwavering support of mentors such as Abdul and Jasmine's mom, how would our journey unfold? There is immense value in recognizing their presence in our lives and expressing gratitude for their guidance and support.

Taking in the teachings of these mentors and letting them

change us can be a big transformation. It's not just about learning from their advice; it's also about holding on to their presence in our lives. When we build quiet confidence, it helps us see things in a stronger, more confident way. This inner strength can then be used to help others. Just like mentors help us grow from small sparks of inspiration, it spreads positivity to those around us when we believe in ourselves and nurture that belief.

My friend is a prime example of this.

A Donated Kidney

Every couple of weeks, my close friend and I head out for a three-to-four-mile walk, starting around 7:00 a.m. and wrapping up by 8:15 a.m. During our walk, we chat about life, ponder deep stuff, support each other, and pray together.

A few months ago, our talks were about a powerful idea—living a life that's not just about us but about making things better for others. What exactly does that mean? How much impact can it have? And how can we actually put this idea into action in our own lives?

What sparked this heart-to-heart was when my friend got a really strong feeling to think about donating one of his kidneys to someone in real need. And guess when this idea hit him? While he was doing pull-ups and messed up his back. Little did he know that this physical setback would start a journey of thinking really deeply. He realized that his body and his life aren't just for him—they can help someone else in a huge way. It was a time of some serious and sort of scary reflection as he thought about how much good he could do by being so selfless.

Talk about diving head first into real, authentic giving and receiving!

Through prayers and the rock-solid support of the people who care about him, my friend felt like he had to explore this path. It meant talking to doctors and getting blood tests and regular checkups to make sure he was mentally and physically ready to give such an important part of himself.

Sure enough, he passed all his tests with flying colors, and this opportunity started to get more real.

He heard about a teenager who needed a kidney, but it turned out that they weren't a match. But he didn't give up. He stayed open to the idea of helping someone else who needed it, believing that if it was meant to be, things would work out.

In an interesting twist, my friend found out about someone nearby who needed a kidney. My friend didn't waste a moment to make a heartfelt call. He asked the person if they'd like his kidney. The person was grateful but said he had already gotten a kidney from a different donor.

And that didn't stop my friend. He kept moving forward with the idea and found out about a 50-year-old man in North Carolina who really needed a kidney. And guess what? That guy ended up receiving my friend's kidney.

Thankfully, the surgery went smoothly, and the three-month recovery was on track.

A few months went by, and my friend was back to normal life. During one of our walks, I got the chance to ask him about the big lessons he learned through this journey. One really important thing he realized was that he had to be open to receiving from others before, during, and after the surgery. He saw that it was a team effort. Even though he was the one who made the call, he knew it involved a lot of people making it happen. One of those people was his wife who did an amazing job holding down the fort at home. And let's not forget the doctors and nurses who ran tests, took care of him, and did the surgery.

He also talked about the strong bond he formed with one of the people who was supposed to get his kidney but didn't. In that experience, there was a real, genuine exchange of giving and receiving. It created a bond of unity that will stick around for a long time.

Behind all this was a mentor my friend gave credit to for guidance and support. That mentor was his higher power—God. While there were others who played a part in his personal and spiritual growth, it was the quiet voice within that led him to the point of realizing, "My life is not just about me anymore."

Regardless of whether we're spiritual, religious, or don't believe in a higher power at all, there's something we can all learn from this. If we're open to mentors, they can truly transform our lives.

When I asked my friend about what he learned in terms of healthy receiving for leaders, he gave two suggestions—which will be in our reflection at the end of this chapter. First, he said it's important to stop and think about what gets in the way of receiving things. That's what we talked about in Chapter 1, "Discover the Power Within for Lasting Success."

We can also consider how we respond and what we express when we have opportunities to receive from others. My friend also emphasized the importance of allowing ourselves to feel a sense of regret. However, that isn't about placing blame on ourselves; it's about becoming aware and stepping into a path of greater freedom.

This deeper understanding of ourselves will push us to receive things in a more meaningful and deep way. It doesn't mean we all need to do something as big as donating a kidney like my friend did. Instead, it's about looking at our life as a flower that needs to be pruned in order to reach its full beauty.

On my friend's amazing journey, he showed that his selfless act was what is possible as a natural result of mentors investing in you. That is how Abdul lived his life. Even though he seemed strong and had a loud voice, he had a quiet confidence that led to a strong, steady belief in making life better for others.

Lesson #7

Silent Strength Radiates

Mentors who bring about big changes notice the inspiration inside us and help it grow stronger. They might spot things in us that we miss and encourage us to show them. They can do that by what they say or what they do. And because of this, the small amount of confidence we had turns into a powerful inner strength that pushes us to do things we wouldn't have done otherwise. That, of course, depends on our willingness to stay open and receptive to what they're sharing.

3 Key Takeaways

1. Looking for mentors who truly have faith in you and can provide helpful guidance, wisdom, and understanding is extremely valuable. Having them around and having their support can shape your path and speed up your personal development.

2. When you build up a calm sense of confidence in yourself, you can see the world in a stronger, more confident way.

3. Quiet confidence makes you believe strongly that you can make good changes in others' lives. It becomes a starting point for making real, positive differences and making important, big changes happen.

Reflection

Mark the words or phrases you often use that prevent you from receiving things. These are statements you say either without realizing it or without thinking. They stop you from genuinely receiving from others. We express some of these statements verbally, while others we keep inside.

To make it easier, I've divided them into three groups.

Praises/Compliments:

- "It was truly a team effort." – Redirecting attention to the team's contribution, highlighting self-lessness.

- "Oh, it was nothing." – Downplaying the accomplishment.

- "Credit goes to a higher power." – Minimizing your partnership with a higher force.

- "Luck played a part; I was fortunate." – Acknowledging external factors without claiming credit.

- "It's just part of my job description." – Minimizing the extraordinary nature based on roles and responsibilities.

- "Anyone would have done the same." – Downplaying the uniqueness of your identity.

- "I believe this is my purpose." – Connecting the

accomplishment to something greater while minimizing personal responsibility.

- "I'm just a work in progress." – Acknowledging room for growth and development while not receiving the joy in where you are today.

Different Perspectives/Opinions:

- "I'm used to my own approach." – Reflecting resistance to change.

- "Old habits die hard." – Indicating a preference for maintaining existing beliefs.

- "I've extensively researched and experienced this." – Sharing expertise while dismissing others' input.

- "I wish they could see things from my point of view." – Expressing a desire for understanding rather than declaring one side as right.

- "I'm familiar with that already." – Acknowledging prior knowledge may assert superiority.

- "Everyone has their own viewpoint." – This often reflects an attitude that discourages going in depth with opposing viewpoints that lead to discussion.

- "They might come to realize it eventually." – This way of thinking gives way to superiority, which undermines healthy learning and different points of view.

- "This has worked for me so far." – Acknowledging a successful approach may diminish other ways of thinking.

Help/Support:

- "I'm fine, no need for help." – Emphasizing self-sufficiency.

- "I appreciate it, but maybe another time." – Leaving room for future assistance while maintaining independence.

- "I've managed on my own so far." – Implying self-reliance and the ability to continue independently.

- "I trust in God's plan." – Combining spirituality with resistance to human support.

- "I don't want to impose on you." – Expressing reluctance to be a burden.

- "I prefer handling things myself." – Associating self-reliance with strength.

- "I can handle things on my own." – Conveying control and resistance to external assistance.

- "There are others who need help more than I do." – Feeling undeserving of assistance and deflecting support to others.

If you want to get better at receiving from others, try taking these 5 steps:

Step 1: Examine the seven primary reasons why receiving can be challenging, as discussed in Chapter 1.

Step 2: Take a moment to reflect on the phrases you frequently use (see above) to deflect or downplay compliments, different perspectives, or help.

Step 3: Acknowledge the specific moments when you may have fallen short in receiving. This is not about self-condemnation but rather an opportunity for growth and fostering a greater sense of freedom and connection.

Step 4: When presented with the opportunity to receive praise, a different perspective, or help from someone, challenge your default response. Take a three-second pause, and then sincerely say, "Thank you! I truly appreciate your taking the time to offer . . ."

Step 5: Within 24 hours of the interaction, set aside time for reflection. Delve deeper into what was said and how you responded, and consider how you can continue to cultivate a more gracious, receptive approach in the future.

By following these steps, you can develop the skill of receiving with greater openness, appreciation, and self-awareness, thus fostering deeper connections and personal growth in your interactions with others.

Part III

Culture Catalyzes Revolution

CHAPTER 8

Kindness in Action

A cup of kindness goes a long way.

—Abdul

After hearing about my professional basketball experience in the last chapter, you may have expected me to keep talking about my time with Abdul into my adult years. But I can't resist sharing one more childhood story that truly shows what kind of person Abdul was.

When each basketball season ended, Abdul and the team had a pizza party as a celebration for each player and the team as a whole. What kid doesn't like that, right?

During the party, our anticipation built up, waiting for Abdul to hand out our basketball report cards, trophies, and other goodies to make us feel extra special.

While parents contributed to purchasing many items, Abdul handcrafted the report cards.

These report cards were completely different from the ones we got at school. They were like night and day in comparison. They were filled with immense detail, creativity, and energy—something that is difficult to put into words.

Every card was a folded piece of white paper, about the size of a regular sheet of paper. Abdul drew the cover on each card. He included things like our team's name (Team Accolade), the year, and each of our names. When we opened the card, there was a lot of interesting stuff inside. It told us about the best players and who had been the most valuable players in the past. It included motivational quotes and even detailed numbers about how well we were doing. Inside the card, Abdul added colorful drawings and pictures that he drew himself. Sometimes he wrote special nicknames for the players, using different colored pens.

This is kindness in action.

Back then, I thought it was a nice thing to do, but now I realize how much it meant. Abdul spent time making these cards just for us, even though we were still young and might not have understood fully. Now that I look back on those times, I see that Abdul was showing me that I was important. He put in the effort to make these special cards, knowing I might not fully get it at the time. As I mentioned last chapter, this is what a mentor does.

They do more than what's expected. They support you no matter what. They are always there for you, and they believe in you even when you're not sure of yourself.

As I write this, I wonder what Abdul was thinking when he made those cards. I still don't fully get it. Maybe other kids just looked at them and threw them away like people sometimes do with birthday cards. But I kept all of them. I never thought I'd be able to show you firsthand what real kindness looks like. Check out the photos below of what these cards looked like.

FRONT	FRONT

FRONT	FRONT

INSIDE	INSIDE

Team - Knicks
Player's Name - Robb Holman (10)
Age - 13   Shoot - Right   Pos. - Guard, Wing, Forward

GP - 15
ST - 136
Sm - 59
A - 78
DR - 37
OR - 12
TR - 49
TO - 66
Ste - 40
Plus or (Minus) - 26
FST - 16
FSm - 11
Fouls - 29
GFD - O
BS - 25
TP - 129

I do think if you stick by your work, believe in yourself, never give up and keep saying to yourself 'I know I'm good - it'll happen. To believe that you have to believe in yourself first and don't look for people to do it for you because if you do, you'll be in real trouble. You have to do it yourself.

I am not what I ought to be, not what I want to be, not what I am going to be but thankful that I am not what I used to be.

When I look around, I always learn something and that is: To be yourself, to express yourself and to have faith in yourself.

You are what you aspire to be and not what you now are, you are what you do with your mind, and you are what you do with your youth.

Chemistry is the blend of players and the main ingredient is unselfishness

The Kindness Club

In an episode of *Inside Out Leadership*, I got to talk to Cheryl Bachelder, a respected servant leader who used to be the CEO of Popeyes Louisiana Kitchen and wrote the book *Dare to Serve: How to Drive Superior Results by Serving Others*. Cheryl shared with me about how important it is to really know and help your team at work. She said leaders should spend a good amount of time each week building relationships and supporting their team.

Cheryl told me about her own experience. She used to focus on this on Mondays and Tuesdays. She set a good example and showed her team that she cares about them. She told leaders to ask their team if they like spending time together and if they really care about how the team is doing. By doing that and spending time with the team, leaders can make their team feel like they matter and are important.

Cheryl also said that when there are problems between coworkers, leaders should ask, "How well do you know the person?" Often, leaders don't know much about their team members' lives outside of work. By showing real interest and asking if anything outside of work is affecting them, leaders can start important conversations that help everyone understand each other better.

As I reflect on the profound impact of Abdul's and Cheryl's kindness, I can't help but envision a world where leaders embrace their principles and join the Kindness

Club. It reminds me of a story about a close friend (the one who donated a kidney) whose daughter led a club called the Kindness Club in her high school. The club's mission was simple yet powerful—to uplift, encourage, and inspire both students and teachers through acts of random kindness to foster a closer-knit school community.

The idea of the Kindness Club extends far beyond high school. It has the potential to revolutionize workplace environments, homes, neighborhoods, and communities worldwide. Imagine if leaders everywhere adopted this principle. Imagine how profoundly it could impact our world and create a sense of unity and connection among people.

Embracing kindness as a leadership practice is not always easy. Kindness requires a shift in mindset and a commitment to consistently practice acts of compassion and understanding. It requires us to set aside our egos, prioritize the well-being of others, and create a culture of kindness in every aspect of our lives.

When we show kindness to others, something magical occurs. It communicates to the person we're being kind to that they hold significance and are genuinely valued. This support acts as a key to help them unlock their beliefs about themselves, others, and the world. The extent to which someone is open to receiving kindness often aligns with their ability to reshape their self-perception.

By increasing our self-kindness, we amplify our capacity to extend kindness to others.

One of the most effective and practical approaches to nurture this quality is taking action toward forgiveness.

Forgiveness Is an Act of Kindness

Have you ever said something you wished you hadn't said, especially to someone important like your child? I recently did just that, and here's what happened next.

After my words hurt my oldest child, I felt bad and apologized right away. But the guilt stayed with me. So the next evening, I asked if we could go for a walk together.

My son agreed, and during that walk, I knew I had to bring up the topic. We stopped, and I looked him in the eyes. I said I was deeply sorry and asked for forgiveness. He said I didn't have to do that since I had already apologized. But I explained that I wanted us to connect honestly and make things right.

At that moment, we had a meaningful talk. I hugged him and shared that making mistakes is part of life. What truly matters is owning up to them and having honest conversations to make things better. I told him kindness is about not just doing right but also about fixing wrongs and showing forgiveness.

During this exchange with my boy, I learned that in seeking forgiveness, I was also forgiving myself. I realized it's never too late to be kind. It might mean planning kindness ahead or quickly forgiving when things go wrong. Either way, showing kindness is a valuable lesson to pass on.

Abdul really knew what he was doing. His handcrafted cards opened up something special in me. It took a while, but those cards made me more open to kindness, both giving and receiving it.

All these examples show that kindness is more than just one thing you do. It's a way of thinking and treating others. Kindness means looking beyond the surface and understanding how others feel. It's about making an effort to lift people up and support them. Whether it's through Abdul's thoughtful cards, Cheryl's way of valuing relationships, or practicing forgiveness, kindness is the heart of living well and getting along with others.

Lesson #8

Kindness in Action

In every little act of kindness, a big kindness tree can grow. Kindness needs us to think differently and keep doing things that show we care and understand. We have to forget about always being right, care more about others, and make kindness a part of everything we do.

When we really practice kindness, it can change everything. It can make offices, homes, neighborhoods, and whole communities much better all around the world.

3 Key Takeaways

1.   Being kind means spending time and paying close attention in order to make something special for someone.

2.   If leaders truly care and ask about personal struggles that might be affecting work, they can start important talks that help everyone understand and care more.

3.   Importance of vulnerability and forgiveness: Admitting our mistakes, seeking forgiveness, and offering grace are vital in cultivating healthy relationships. Being open and vulnerable allows for deeper connections and fosters growth within ourselves and our interactions with others.

Reflection

- It's time to build and foster your Kindness Club!

- What are you willing to commit to in the next 30 days (formally or informally) to uplift, encourage, and inspire your team members through acts of random kindness in order to foster a closer-knit workplace or community?

CHAPTER 9

Compassion-Driven Collaboration

Chemistry is the unique blend of players, and the main ingredient is unselfishness.

—*Abdul*

Years ago, I started something really meaningful to me—a community church that welcomed people of all different backgrounds. Our first public service was something to remember. It kicked off a movement that brought people together, both locally and globally, with excitement in their hearts.

About six months later, we had a special Easter service that I remember well. Easter represents hope and strength during tough times, no matter what you believe.

That Easter service was even more important to me because Abdul was there supporting me. Abdul was Muslim but wasn't super religious. He came to our big gathering not because he shared my beliefs but to show that he cared about what was important to me. Abdul was open to learning from my world, even though it was different from his.

Since he couldn't drive, Abdul came with a mutual friend of ours. During the service, I had many things to do—meet new people, teach, and make everyone feel welcome. Sadly, I never got a chance to tell Abdul how much his being there meant to me that day.

As a young pastor with a growing church, I knew that having someone believe in me was huge. It's nice when people who believe the same things as you support you, but it's really something special when someone believes in you as a person.

Abdul's presence at the Easter service without any obligation showed how strong support can be. His being there meant more than words can say. It reminded me that real support goes beyond having the same beliefs—it comes from truly believing in each other.

Today, I think back to Abdul and how much he influenced me. I'm thankful for his presence on that Easter Sunday, a day of hope, renewal, and the power of working together for good.

What you might need to know is that there was one other service Abdul participated in about three years before that also contributed to this process.

It was the day Karen and I got married.

We planned our wedding for seven months, and as you can imagine, we were beyond excited for the special day. Deciding who to invite was tough, but one person had to come—Abdul.

As beautiful and memorable as our wedding ceremony was, what made our day even better was watching Abdul at the reception. We played a lot of dance music from the 1950s and 1960s. Karen and I love that music, but I think Abdul loved it even more.

With our closest family members and friends there, the atmosphere was electric! For most of the reception, people were out of their seats and joining in on all the fun.

And guess who danced the most? Abdul! He danced in a very carefree way, not worried about time and just having fun.

On our important day, my mentor and friend danced with us. I can still see him dancing, getting sweaty under his arms. Abdul's presence at our wedding made our day really, really special. I have a recording of that day and those special moments, and I'll keep it always.

Abdul was very impressive at both the wedding and the Easter service. Let's be honest, when you think about taking part in a service or event for someone with different beliefs, faith, or opinions, it can feel . . .

. . . awkward.

. . . challenging.

. . . stressful.

That's because it's not what we're used to. "Different" doesn't mean "wrong." It just means "not the same." Sometimes there are cultural or special ceremonies we're not familiar with. Often it's easier for people who don't share your beliefs to not come at all. And even if they do come, they might not join in because it's different for them.

Abdul showed how he could be part of different situations, even if he didn't believe the same things. His strong belief in me and his choice to join in showed how important it is to support and connect with others, even when we're different. That made those moments truly amazing.

Expanding Our Understanding

I once got to talk with Kimberly Loh, a specialist in solving conflicts and negotiating globally. I was doing a series of interviews with leaders who look inside themselves in order to lead better. Kim talked about how her mixed background shaped her. Her family is from places such as Malaysia and Singapore, and she grew up in the United Kingdom, Hong Kong, and Singapore. Because of that, she understands and cares about lots of cultures and beliefs. She's like a peacemaker in her own life. She sees the different stories, the hopes, and the ways people show who they are.

Kim said it's important to see both the good and the not-so-good when cultures mix. That helped her see more, appreciate more, and be open to learning from anyone, anywhere. In her book *Compassionate Conversations*, she talks about how a lot of the world's problems come from people not understanding each other's identities.

She thinks it's important that we don't just think about our own group. We need to get into other people's shoes and really understand where they're coming from. That helps us respect others and not judge them based on our ideas about them. Remember when I talked about this in Chapter 2, "Embrace Your Inner North Star"?

Abdul knew his identity and was committed to learning mine too. He also showed how to live and lead this way, but he didn't have to go all around the world to receive it. He just cared about the people right around him and focused on those nearby. Perhaps that is the main reason he never got a driver's license. He was content with his local area and the people who resided in it. He learned from them, believed in them, and united them for a shared goal.

This is compassion-driven collaboration.

The Power of Caring Collaboration

The study "Caring and Task Involvement: Provider Role Perceptions, Emotion, and Collaboration in Health Care Teams" by Fisher, Caron, and Hajdaj looks at how being caring and focused on tasks affects teamwork in healthcare groups. They saw that when people care and are involved in tasks, they think better of each other's roles. It makes them feel more positive and work together better. The study shows that in order for teams to work well, we need to think about both the jobs we do and how we feel, especially in healthcare. This means that when team members care about each other and the work they do, they can help patients more.

Kimberly Loh's ideas and Abdul's way of living are like what the study found. Kim talks about how we should listen to different views and not just stick to our own way of thinking. When we really get into someone else's shoes and see things their way, we can treat them better and without judgment. Doing that helps teams work together better.

"Coach Dad" Learns an Invaluable Lesson

My daughter Kayla and I never miss our basketball workouts, rain or shine. We believe tough conditions make us stronger and more resilient. But recently, something was off. I could see Kayla wasn't herself. Her usual energy was gone.

As "Coach Dad," I felt I should push her like an elite athlete. Maybe it was my training kicking in during all those years of playing pro ball or just a dad who wanted to instill perseverance in a rising superstar daughter. Either way, I thought pushing through tough times was the way to go. But Kayla felt pressured, and the more I pushed, the less she cared.

Her shots weren't good, her passes were off, and she was really struggling. Things got tense, and she got frustrated and even cried. I realized we both needed a break.

I told Kayla I'd step back and let her be. So I went inside the house and watched to see what she would do on her own. My hope was that if I wasn't there, it would be better, but it only got worse. Her frustration increased, and the tears came even more.

Watching this, I felt the need to make a change. So I went back out and suggested that we do the drills together. The moment I mentioned it, her face lit up with excitement. Being with her through the challenges turned out to be much better than stepping away or even helping from the side. We dribbled side by side and felt a deep sense of connection. Her energy shifted, and as a natural byproduct, her skills improved.

Importantly, I didn't suggest this change so she would perform better. It came from a deeper place in me that wanted to share her burden in order to ease her discouragement, frustration, and sadness.

The most wonderful part was how much closer we became in that moment. As Coach Dad, sharing the challenge made our bond stronger. Her skills got better, and I received a gift that day too.

It reminded me of how Abdul lived. He joined me in my biggest moments, no matter our differences or how he felt. He believed in sharing life with others as he built trust and connection.

So who's your "Kayla"? Who needs more than advice? Step in, and be there whether it's someone on your team or in your family. Sharing their journey helps everyone grow. Trust builds, and together we achieve more.

Don't just watch. Stand with your "Kayla," and be part of their journey. You'll be amazed at how much both of you change and achieve. The impact you create by being there lasts a lifetime.

Lesson #9

Compassion-Driven Collaboration

You might not share the same beliefs, opinions, or experiences as someone else, but believing in that person is truly valuable. It produces more compassion and helps you connect and receive from others in meaningful, powerful ways.

3 Key Takeaways

1.   True support goes beyond shared beliefs. It stems from a genuine belief in each other.

2.   There is an opportunity to fully inhabit each unique perspective in the present moment without becoming bound by it.

3.   When we actively participate in others' journeys, there is tremendous potential for compassion-driven collaboration.

Reflection

- Think about someone in your life who needs more than just distant cheers or outside help. It could be someone on your team or in your family. Once you figure out who it is, find a way to truly "join in" with them by doing something practical together.

- Think about someone who sees things differently than you—maybe about business, ideas, politics, or anything else. When you meet them next time, really listen and show interest in their story. Don't try to prove them wrong, but open your heart to understand their perspective. Remember, this means you need you to listen carefully and aim to understand, not just to win an argument.

CHAPTER 10

Altruistic Leadership Wave

Man is always thought of as greater and more important than the state, but he is never thought of as greater and more important than the family because apart from the family, he has no real existence.

—*Abdul*

"He passed away just over a year ago," the police officer told me, delivering news that shook me to my core. "No way. This can't be true," I responded.

I found out this unbelievable news after running into a local policeman who had attended one of my training sessions. When I learned he was from the same town as Abdul, I had felt compelled to ask how Abdul was doing.

And then he told me. All at once, questions flooded my mind.

How did I not realize the seriousness of Abdul's condition?

Why was I unaware of his memorial service?

Why didn't I ever let him know the profound impact he had on my life?

Picture trying to lead the training session for another two hours while these questions (and more) echoed through my heart and mind.

What I did know was that Abdul had experienced a stroke about six years before he passed away. I realized that I hadn't seen him since that initial Easter service I mentioned in the previous chapter. And I hadn't spoken to him since his stroke. My family and I often talked about how meaningful it would be to pay him a visit. But then life took its course, and we got caught up in the busyness of life's demands. To be honest, maybe it was the case of a little "out of sight, out of mind."

A few months after I heard the news that Abdul had passed away, I ran into an old friend at a local high school basketball game. He was one of the guys who was on some of those smelly car rides to various tournaments. When I asked if he knew Abdul had passed away, he went on to share his experience of attending the memorial service. He was deeply moved by how the local community united to provide overwhelming support for Abdul's family during the service. All the expenses were covered by everyone in the community. And a large number of people came together to honor his memory and celebrate his life. "It was truly something special," my old friend told me.

Yet I was absent. Once more, a series of questions rushed into my mind.

To be honest, I'm still unpacking a lot of what transpired, even though it's been over three years now! From the outset, I started this book project with the intention of honoring Abdul. My goal was to share the milestones and lessons I'd gathered that have truly reshaped my life and leadership. But there's more to it. This book has also given me a remarkable platform to navigate through the grieving journey. It really depends on the day. Sometimes an overwhelming sadness takes hold. Other days, I regret that I should have visited him more. On other days, I find myself laughing out loud at a memory of something he said to me or a gesture he made.

One thing it has revealed to me is that grief can carry a deep sadness mingled with profound appreciation. I found comfort in the lessons Abdul gave me, lessons that transformed my life in immeasurable ways. It was as if a floodgate had opened, releasing a wave of memories, teachings, and moments of growth we had shared together.

Maybe I started to fully understand the importance of receiving help and support during this huge loss. I also felt regret for not saying goodbye to Abdul and expressing how much he truly meant to me. I wish I could have let him know how grateful I was for who he was and the valuable lessons he taught me.

This heartbreaking news marked the beginning of a journey—a journey of mourning and honor that flows through the pages of this book. Each word, each reflection is an attempt to pay tribute to the profound impact Abdul had on my life and the lives of countless others. It is a testament to the enduring influence of a mentor, a friend, and a guiding light.

Ride the Wave

What can we learn about receiving? The final lesson Abdul left me revolves around embracing the wave of selfless leadership, something I like to call the "Altruistic Leadership Wave." This type of leadership involves guiding others with the genuine intention of enhancing their well-being. It comes from a place of caring for others and a sincere desire to assist, devoid any sense of obligation, loyalty, or religious pressure.

When you truly internalize the nine lessons of this book and put them into practice, you naturally ride the wave of serving others selflessly and sincerely. This isn't about serving out of duty or trying to meet expectations. It's about aligning your actions with your authentic self. There are no conditions or demands attached to your efforts. Imagine if everyone received in a manner that en-

abled them to give from that same pure place. The result would be a wondrous exchange of humanity!

Abdul embodied this spirit. Whenever I was with him, I never sensed any ulterior motives or hidden agendas. He gave freely from a place deep within his heart, just as he had received in a similarly genuine manner. I often wonder where he learned these lessons—perhaps from faith, from his upbringing, from his time in the Vietnam War. Or maybe it was his appreciation for old music. But regardless of the source, what kept his flame burning was his unwavering commitment to learning. No matter his location or the company he kept, he remained a student, consistently passing on the wisdom he had gained and thus transforming the lives around him.

When we truly receive and live in this manner, we can share it with others. It's like catching a massive wave at the beach. I used to love body surfing on the shores of New Jersey. Well, between you and me, I still do! There's an incredible thrill in seeking out the biggest wave, timing it just right, and riding it all the way to shore. In a similar vein, we can help ourselves and others catch the immense wave of altruistic leadership. But here's the twist. It's not a wave you catch on the outside; it's one you catch on the inside and then let it work its magic outwardly.

Looking back, Abdul's impact on me might have been bigger than I realized. Imagine this. Right after college, while I was chasing my dream of playing pro basketball, I started running inspirational basketball camps for kids ages 5 to 14.

During this journey, I partnered with my older brother, Scott. We weren't just teaching basketball basics; we were using the game to impart invaluable life lessons to kids. We did it all—coaching them one-on-one, holding fun camps and clinics, organizing leagues, and even giving motivational talks at local schools.

Two years after starting this business, my brother and

I took a step further and acquired a basketball clothing brand. That allowed us to extend our coaching philosophy through our brand, reaching and influencing kids across the entire United States. And guess what? Before I turned 23, my brother and I had not just one but two incredibly significant organizations. And even while chasing my dream of playing pro basketball, I kept pushing forward.

This whole thing kick-started my journey as a business owner. Over the next 26 years, I got to start or help start nine different companies. It's like I caught this exciting wave, all because—just like Abdul—I really wanted to help people. Everything I did, I saw it as a way to make a difference.

No Strings Attached

During a recent interview with my good friend and top engagement influencer Marcel Schwantes, he discussed servant leadership and unconditional love.

Marcel talked about the need to practice unconditional love at home and in business. It entailed focusing on others' needs without expecting anything in return. This approach is not transactional—there are no strings attached. Interestingly, when you genuinely care for people and meet their needs unconditionally, they naturally respond in ways that benefit both parties.

In the context of marriage, meeting your partner's needs fosters intimacy. Your partner seeks emotional connection and vulnerability, which creates closeness for them. On the other hand, you have a different need for fun and adventure. When they express love by participating in activities you enjoy, it fills you with happiness. Over the course of your multi-year marriage, you discover how to love each other unconditionally, which results in genuine fulfillment for both of you.

Marcel's emphasis on unconditional love and servant leadership reinforces the importance of selflessly serving others, caring for their needs, and building genuine connections. It resonates with the idea of "catching the wave" of altruistic leadership.

One thing I would like to highlight in line with Marcel's encouragement is that the more you embrace and receive unconditional love, the more you can naturally give it to others. It may come as a surprise, but giving from this place of unconditional love becomes a powerful byproduct of receiving it. In other words, when you allow yourself to receive deeply, you find yourself naturally catching the wave of altruistic leadership.

Putting in effort, staying focused, and being intentional and consistent remain essential. Yet rather than pushing forcefully, let it flow naturally. Let "the music find you" and engage your senses. Your capacity to give back stems from the positive contributions you've accumulated over your lifetime. When you truly receive and wholeheartedly embrace unconditional love, giving becomes a spontaneous overflow of that very same love.

One Chapter Ends, Another Begins

A few years ago, I found myself on the edge of a major milestone in my life. My youngest child, Zach, was nearing his preschool graduation—a moment that stirred up many emotions within me and my wife. It wasn't just about celebrating this special milestone in my son's life; it symbolized the culmination of a chapter, a season that brought finality to our family life. It wasn't only about celebrating my son's special moment; it was like reaching the end of a part in our family's story, like closing a chapter on something important.

As the days drew closer to graduation day, a sense of anticipation began to well up within me. I must admit that I was more than a little nervous, maybe even a bit more nervous than giving a keynote in front of a thousand people. Unlike the confidence I have in my profession, the nerves were due to heading in some uncharted territory.

The big day had finally arrived, and along with the other parents, my wife and I were bursting with pride. And why wouldn't we be? Zach is one of the most thoughtful, dedicated, and enjoyable people you'll ever meet. And he really enjoys school! Karen couldn't stop smiling, and I found myself talking more than usual because I was so excited.

The graduation ceremony lasted a mere 30 minutes. There were a few songs, some inspiring words, and, of course, Zach's big walk across a tiny bridge—an act that symbolized the end of one season and the dawn of a new one. In our role as proud parents, we couldn't help but soak in every moment, and we took dozens of photos and videos.

However, what truly caught us off guard was a heart-felt acknowledgement from his teacher as the ceremony drew to a close. She surprised us by recognizing our family's journey through preschool, not just with Zach but with all three of our children. The teachers honored us for our unwavering commitment to each of our children during their final year of preschool.

This meant no more preschool, ever again.

In that present moment, it dawned on me that I wasn't merely enjoying Zach's accomplishments. I was also reflecting on the closing of a chapter in my own life and the opening of a new one. Seasons of service may be revealed in different ways, but what remains constant is a life dedicated to serving others.

As I look back on Zach's graduation and the end of this specific period, it brings to mind how crucial it is to welcome every chapter, treasure the moments, and acknowledge the valuable lessons they carry.

Abdul's passing marked the beginning of a chapter that continues to unfold, a chapter filled with introspection, growth, and a commitment to honor his memory.

A Way of Thinking That Inspires Your Future

It has always intrigued me that when someone passes away or a chapter of life concludes, we not only grieve the loss but also what that person or season represented to us. However, I've discovered that when I reflect on these things with a heart full of gratitude, new life emerges from the midst of loss. That is how it's been since I heard the news about Abdul. It doesn't mean we completely move on, but it can propel us into a new chapter, building upon the lessons of the past. This mindset becomes a source of inspiration for our future.

Consider this age-old question: *Is your glass half empty or half full?*

In a recent poll I conducted, 19% of the people identified as pessimistic, 70% as optimistic, and 11% as other. A pessimistic person tends to expect the worst in any situation, while an optimistic person anticipates a positive outcome in the future. Now let's imagine that a challenging event occurs. The pessimistic person might say, "I told you so!" while the optimistic person may say, "Tomorrow will be a brighter day!" Who is right?

Perhaps it's not about being right or wrong but rather about allowing our reality to inspire our future. Ronald Siegel once said, "It's one thing to think positively about your future and another to be inspired by reality."

This is where present thinking comes into play. By anchoring ourselves in the present reality, acknowledging

our real-time feelings, and simultaneously embracing a state of gratitude—even in challenging circumstances—we naturally pave the way for a positive outcome.

In the midst of my grief, I discovered a renewed sense of purpose—to preserve Abdul's memory, to honor his legacy, and to share the invaluable wisdom he gave me. Through the act of writing, I not only navigate my feelings but also celebrate the immense value he added to my life.

This book serves as a tribute—an outpouring of gratitude for the lessons I learned, the insights I gained, and the transformative experiences Abdul and I shared. It is a testament to the power of human connection and the profound mark one person can leave on another's life.

As I reflect on the impact of Abdul's lessons, I am reminded of the importance of cherishing those who have touched our lives. Their influence extends far beyond their physical presence. Though Abdul may no longer be with us, his spirit lives on in the memories we hold dear and the lessons we carry within us.

Now, as I reminisce about the moment I first walked into that gym and heard Abdul's booming voice and felt intimidated, I'm no longer nervous, apprehensive, or fearful. Instead, I'm filled with excitement, confidence, and courage. This transformation was a genuine partnership. It started with a man who was quite different from me, someone with so much to give. And it extended to a young boy who was willing to open himself up and receive. Because of this real and honest exchange of giving and receiving, Abdul took me under his wing and uncovered the hidden power of receiving from anyone, anytime. The gift I've been given I now give to you.

Perhaps this is why I'm contemplating the idea of coaching basketball—again. Only time will tell. One thing is for sure. I can hear Abdul say, "Greyhound, don't overthink it!"

Lesson #10

Catch the Altruistic Leadership Wave

The last lesson Abdul imparted was about embracing the wave of selfless leadership. When you truly receive by practicing the nine previous lessons, you effortlessly catch the current of serving others unconditionally and with genuine intentions. It's not about serving out of obligation or meeting expectations. You do it because it aligns with your authentic self. When you do, influence results in lasting impact. I'm a living example of that!

3 Key Takeaways

1. It's not just okay to grieve; it's necessary.

2. There is power in unconditional love.

3. If we remain open to receive, the chapters of life can offer transformative wisdom.

Reflection

- Who is an unconventional mentor you've had, and what transformative lessons did they teach you?

- If that mentor is still alive, what can you do to express your gratitude privately or publicly? If they have passed away, how can you honor their legacy?

- What is your most significant takeaway from *Lessons from Abdul*, and how can you apply it practically in the next 30 days?

Conclusion

As I stand before a mirror, an image comes into view.

At first, it's hard to recognize because it seems like me, yet with every glance, the familiar me fades, and a new version emerges. It's almost like the flicker of a light bulb when it turns on.

I'm taken aback by this new image, although not entirely surprised.

With each passing moment, the new image becomes clearer, gradually revealing itself. It's drawing me in— in ways I'd never feel drawn to my own reflection.

As I continue to look, feelings of love, worth, and meaning well up within me.

I've almost disappeared, and this new image has fully captured my attention. The flicker of the light bulb has transformed into a steady, bright glow.

It's truly beautiful beyond description.

This person represents all those who long for your presence.

In other words, when you embrace your unique identity,

you start to see things from a higher perspective. Life isn't just about you; it's about others.

As I discover or rediscover who I am, I feel compelled to serve those around me faithfully. This is what I call Inside Out Leadership.

Remember, you can only give what you have received. When you fully receive your true self, you can act from a place of freedom and openness in order to serve others selflessly.

This is what Abdul taught me—how to receive deeply in order to give greatly.

From the outside, it might have seemed like Abdul had little, but inside he was rich. That's because he could receive, and that allowed him to give generously. The most incredible part is that Abdul didn't need to see many of the results in others' lives since he knew the seeds he planted would bloom, even if he wasn't around to see it.

Now it's your turn to embrace your true self and make the most of your potential in helping others.

Who are you? Why are you here?

Let the beauty and strength of your identity take over as you embrace your unique purpose.

In memory of . . .

Abdul Ford-Bey

October 3, 1947 – July 23, 2018

Acknowledgments

I extend my deepest thanks to my mom, June, and dad, Bob, for showing me the importance of learning from those who are different from me and for welcoming Abdul into our lives.

I'm also grateful to my brother, Scott, and sister, Laurie, for joining me in the experiences we've shared with Abdul.

Special thanks go to my chief editor, Sue, and my editing team - Fred, Chris, and Scott - for helping me shine.

I want to express my immense appreciation to my graphic designer, Asim, book layout designer, Daria, and my video editor, Jesse, for your incredible creativity.

A heartfelt thank you to my wife, Karen, and my three wonderful kids - RJ, Kayla, and Zach - for your unwavering support and encouragement throughout this very important project.

LEARN MORE ...

Robb Holman is an internationally recognized leadership keynote speaker and trainer who helps audiences connect with their unique life's purpose and find success in a way they never expected—from the inside out!

If you're interested in having Robb give a passionate keynote talk or experiential training workshop on *Lessons from Abdul* or learn more about his Inside Out Leadership™ products and services, visit:

www.robbholman.com

Robb's Books

Lead the Way: Inside Out Leadership Principles for Business Owners & Leaders
www.LeadTheWayBook.com

All In: How Impactful Teams Build Trust from the Inside Out
www.GetAllInBook.com

Move the Needle: How Inside Out Leaders Influence Organizational Culture

www.MoveTheNeedleBook.com

Lessons from Abdul: The Hidden Power of Receiving from Anyone, Anytime

www.LessonsFromAbdul.com

To Interact with Robb, visit:

Twitter: www.twitter.com/robbholman

Facebook: www.facebook.com/robbholman1

LinkedIn: www.linkedin.com/in/robbholman

YouTube: www.youtube.com/c/robbholman

Instagram: www.instagram.com/robb.holman

Clubhouse: www.joinclubhouse.com/@robbholman

POSITIVE. PASSIONATE. POWERFUL.

RH ROBB HOLMAN
INSIDE OUT LEADERSHIP

ROBB HOLMAN

is an internationally recognized leadership expert, executive coach, keynote speaker, podcast co-host, and bestselling author who has a heart for authentic relationships and a true talent for equipping people with the skills and the knowledge necessary for their success. His work has been featured in top publications like Inc., Forbes, and Fast Company and endorsed by many of the world's top leadership thinkers.

http://www.robbholman.com/speaking

 Robb.holman

 Robbholman1

 Robbholman

 @Robbholman

Robb is a charismatic and dynamic speaker who has the ability to capture an audience from the moment he speaks. You can tell by his presence the passion he has for his business and his leadership. I would highly recommend Robb for any speaking engagements. The take-away knowledge and inspiration for your audience is abundant.

— Carla Haydt

 www.robbholman.com   484.401.7966   info@robbholman.com

Three Important Deliverables Coming Out Of This Course

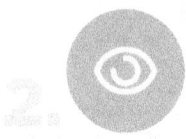

DISCOVER YOUR BIG WHY   **DEVELOP YOUR BIG VISION**   **DEFINE YOUR BUSINESS PLAN**

Robb's Inside Out Leadership Academy is now available through his global consultancy, Holman International, to bring you the best of Inside Out Leadership™ Online!

Robb Holman presents his proven and purposeful Inside Out Leadership™ principles as a practical guide to transform your leadership and help you LEAD THE WAY!

www.robbholman.com   484.401.7966   info@robbholman.com

142

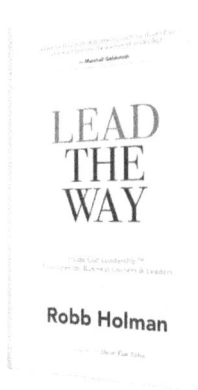